The Illusion of School

The Real Reason Why Children Fail

By

Roy Andersen

The Moving Quill Publishing House.

MQ

Copyright © Roy Andersen. 2013

The right of Roy Andersen to be identified as the author of this work has been asserted by him in accordance with the Copyright Designs and Patents Act 1988. This work is registered with UK Copyright Service Registration No. 284678360.

All rights reserved. No part of this publication may be reproduced, stored in a retrieval system, or transmitted, in any form or by any means, electronic, mechanical, photocopying, recording, or otherwise, without the prior written permission of the copyright owner.

Disclaimer:

The author and the publisher will assume no liability nor responsibility to any person or entity with respect to any loss or damage related directly or indirectly to the information in this book. Neither the author nor the publisher will provide any remedy for indirect, consequential, punitive, or incidental damages arising from this book, including such from negligence, strict liability, or breach of warranty or contract, even after notice of the possibility of such damages. Neither the publisher nor the author accept any responsibility for the actions of another based on the information in this book.

ISBN: 9780995610606

I would like to dedicate this book

to

My daughters Gini and Naomi who never stopped believing in me

and

who may everything possible.

Acknowledgements

There is not space here to mention all the many people I have ironed out my thoughts with in the twenty years it took me to complete these books. To those I mention here, and to many others, I am profoundly grateful for their time, generosity, and the great friendship they have shown me.

Prof. / Dean Emeritus. David Martin. Gallaudet University. U.S.A.
Prof. Søren Nørby. Denmark.
Prof. Mads Hermansen. Nordic School of Public Health. Sweden.
Prof. Freddy Bugge Christiansen. Arhus University. Denmark.
Prof. Albert Gjedde. Arhus University Hospital. Denmark.
Prof. Rik Drummond-Brydson. Leeds University. England.
Prof. Jorn Bundgaard Nielsen. Arhus University. Denmark.
Dr. Paul Harris. Southern College of Optometry. U.S.A.
Dr. Abdelkader Makhlouf El Bayadh University Algeria
Prof. Cosimo Di Magli. The Anne Frank School. Italy.
Prof. Harry Chugani. Wayne State University. U.S.A.
Prof. Laming. Cambridge University. England.
Prof. Luca Magni. LUISS Business School. Italy

Prof. Martha Constanine-Paton. MIT. U.S.A.
Prof. Carla Shatz. Stanford University. U.S.A.
Prof. Derek Forest. Dublin University. Ireland.
Ms. Claudia Krenz. U.S.A.
Ms. Leigh Collinge. Australia.
Ms. Sara Lappi. U.S.A.

PREFACE

It will probably take a few years, possibly even a decade before the public at large will get how revolutionary the ideas of Roy Andersen are.

His ideas resonate perfectly with the Learnable Theory and are destined to impact not only teaching in schools, but also the way human resources are selected and developed in organizations. Indeed, Roy's deconstruction of intelligence goes well beyond Daniel Coleman, Howard Gardner and what others have done so far. Roy goes at the root of learning, he links it to the creation and leveraging of meanings and how the symbolic process of language plays a key role in what we generally identify and name intelligence.

It is for these reasons that I am inclined to believe that Roy's ideas have the potential to promote a major turn around in all the multiple educational fields and practices, including Managerial Sciences.

Professor Luca Magni. LUISS Business School.

Rome. Italy

Table of Contents

Introduction	ix
Chapter One: The Role of Education	3
Chapter Two: The Bell Curve	21
Chapter Three: The Scheme of Things	36
Chapter Four: To understand the whole as of parts	45
Chapter Five: The Individual and Their Intelligence	58
Chapter Six: The Importance of Words	70
Chapter Seven: The Individual and School	81
Chapter Eight: A System for the Masses	97
Chapter Nine: The Modeling of Society Members	108
Chapter Ten: The Evolvement of Education	120
Chapter Eleven: Education: From What and To Where	134
Chapter Twelve: Digital Interference	140
Chapter Thirteen: The Mind of the Student	147
Chapter Fourteen: The Effect of Bullying or Social Humiliation	166
Chapter Fifteen: The Rules of Learning	172
Chapter Sixteen: The Art of Sensitivity in Awareness	187
Chapter Seventeen: Ben Learns How to Get Better Grades in School	207
Chapter Eighteen: A Guide to Better Teaching	219
Chapter Nineteen: The Future Role of Education	226
Books by Roy Andersen	244
Illustrations	250
References	251

A Personal Introduction by Roy Andersen

A new type of thinking is essential if mankind is to survive and move toward higher levels.

Albert Einstein

Before we begin the actual book, I would like to give an extended summary of some of the important things it will discuss. Because the book offers to rewrite very much of what we know, I wish to explain its overall content clearly. Therefore, with your agreement, I would like to begin by asking the question:

Why don't all children gain top marks?

All, if not most, parents want this for their child. All, if not most, employers desire the school to provide future workers who are more competent and more adaptable to learn new skills, as demonstrated by higher grades. All, if not most, teachers wish their students would respond in the right ways at the right times to give all top marks, but they don't. Students vary in their effort, interests, drives, and abilities.

Governments, corporations, psychologists, educators, and numerous individuals have invested enormous amounts of money, time, and energy to create better learning environments in the expectation, if not hope, that students will learn better and gain better grades, but they don't. New gurus are endlessly presented to inspire teachers with new methods to make learning better. Teachers like these. Students like them, but no change in ability is witnessed.

Students still vary as they always have done in a class. One or two know the correct answers and always gain the top marks. One or two seem to understand nothing, and the rest struggle in between, hoping they will be better graded, but never understand why they are not. Despite all the effort put into education, the general performance of students really does not change.

Throughout 12 years of schooling, I was one of the worst in my class. I never understood what I did wrong to always gain low marks and seemingly more red scribbles than anyone else. At 17, I failed all my final school examinations. Yet, I went back into education at 20 and achieved tremendous academic success. All my examination results were graded the very highest.

Since then, and in different guises, I have struggled over the past 40 years to find out what is wrong with the ways school operates. My motivation was that I never wanted one child to fail as I had done. I created this to be my life's mission. It took me decades to really discover what is wrong with school. In this book, I share some of my findings with you.

One of the first things we need to realise is that, while different countries create different political designs for the education of their children, they are all built upon the same basic 19th-century purpose. This is to produce the managers and the managed who maintain the operation of the society.

While these political designs play to the apparent social background of children with different purposes, there are numerous strategies, some obvious and others not so, that are encoded into the schools of every country. These strategies are designed to promote a certain stability in society. So that, in general, children follow the work level of their parents, enabling the social organisation to maintain a sense of order. We will examine how changes in technology impact this design. However, this design gives the intended impression that the abilities of students and the grades they earn are based on their abilities, rather than the responsibility of education itself.

This ability is partially attributed to the child's upbringing, but more significantly to the quality of intelligence they inherited. From this understanding, each child has a certain but predetermined latitude for how they may develop through the learning environment.

This is to say that if you give exactly the same information to two students, the one who inherited better genes will more likely obtain the better result. In other words, children are born with different intelligences. This belief is the foundation of the reasoning why some students gain better grades than others.

It took me some 40 years to complete my book "Intelligence: The Great Lie". After it had been published, the dean of an American university stated that this was one of the most important books published this century. You see, the book explains how the concept of an inherited intelligence was manufactured as a political mechanism in the 19th century, to create a mindset that social ranking was a consequence of inherited natural ability.

The science of psychology grew out of this belief, and through questionable data, fraud, and even lies, psychologists have ever since convinced society that intelligence is, in some part, inherited and measurable. The aforementioned book explains in depth why a quality of intelligence is not inherited and why intelligence cannot be measured, such that the IQ is a fallacy.

Yet, since what I state here goes against 150 years of traditional understanding that intelligence is inherited, I had to qualify my belief that it is not inherited through many years of research in genetics and neurology. It was only through this that I came to realise that all that is inherited is the ability to be intelligent and that the quality an individual has of intelligence is one developed through the environment.

The environment, however, is far, far more complex than it is understood to be by psychologists, who try to define the life experiences of an individual, for their genetic value of intelligence to be evaluated. The simple reality is that because of the unfathomable depth of the environment of any individual, it can never be known. Consequently, the genetic value of their intelligence can also never be known. Therefore, the reasoning that all normally born students in education have different qualities of intelligence has no scientific foundation.

This is to say that children ARE born with equal abilities to develop their intelligence, unless, of course, they inherited genes that affect the development of their nervous system, such as Huntington's disease, a chromosomal mutation at conception, causing, for example, Down Syndrome, or incurred some pre-birth complications, such as oxygen starvation. All of these produce visible signs in the human child, which allow us to recognize that they need a special education to help them develop better in a normal environment.

It took Nancy Bayley 50 years to complete her testing on 50,000 infants before she testified that there is no definable difference in the intelligence of infants until they reach 14 months of age. Therefore, there is no evidence that gene codes are responsible for the intelligence of normally born children. The belief that they are is simply based on a 19th-century political design.

In fact, Bayley further stated that whatever intelligence was assigned to a child after 14 months, that this value could be directly related to the ways of those who raised them. She further found that whatever intelligence is thought of a child at 5, 6, or 7 years of age, that this impression could be radically changed once they had finished their education.

Therefore, if normal children, born with exactly the same opportunities for intelligence, continually produce stable differences in their school performance, what causes this? And why has education never found the means for all students to perform equally?

It is easier to answer the second question than the first, because education has a mandate to provide variations of ability to match the variations of capability the working sector requires. After all, competitive private schools and government schools, and so the path in life each provides for their students.

One less obvious strategy lies in the tactics developed within the school system to hamper the efficiency and energy of the teacher. First, by the way they were educated to be teachers, with a focus on improving the knowledge of the inherited brain, rather than the environmental mind, and thus less aware of how to stimulate student awareness and confidence. Then, by the administrative tasks that drain their energies for the classes they teach, in which too many students do not understand what they should have been confident with in previous years, as a consequence of how earlier teachers taught them. This has led to teachers being exhausted and drained by their working conditions, with the consequence that many now leave their profession at an alarming rate.

Teacher retention is now a serious problem within education, which it attempts to compensate for by increasing computer-based learning, without understanding the social problems this breeds. Children who learn through computers and less through social interaction tend to be self-centered and narcissistic. This has led to increases in cyberbullying, which deeply affects the ability of more children to learn. Yet, all we have just uncovered fades into insignificance when we discover how school really works.

A very defining strategy, which is very well hidden, is for the school not to educate students in reason, which (setting aside attempts to teach critical thinking, which is ineffectively taught), it has never been done, and leaves the responsibility for this to the ways different parents raise their children. It is only students who move to the university level who gain this education in reason, for the greater responsibility they will take in the running of their society. Therefore, by neglecting formal education in reason at the school level, society fosters a natural disparity in parents with different awarenesses of how to raise their children.

So, we find that parents who are aware of higher language and better thinking skills, often having had a university education themselves, seem to naturally raise their children with the skills that enable their children to perform better in school and so move to the university. In contrast, parents who were deprived of a university education and so unaware of these skills, and who are encouraged to believe the school will teach their children to learn, raise their children with poor qualities, for the school experience, compared to those children who were better prepared, and so often fail to gain the grades to go to university.

Indeed, Hart and Risley made a great deal of research in 1995 to demonstrate how the performance of 10-year-old children in school was strongly related to the language skills they were raised under in the first 3 years of life. These researchers were able to confirm that this zero-to-three-year timeframe was related to the language skills of parents, as a projection of their socio-economic status.[1] In other words, how well the parents raised their children on stories and explained in great detail the world about them, so their children developed very high language skills, which later played a decisive role in the grades they obtained in school.

There is open acknowledgement that Finnish schools are the best in the world. However, the Finnish teachers I have talked to argued against this, but stressed how the Finnish social system encourages parents to know how to better prepare their child for school, which their school system builds upon. For example, when a mother gives birth in Finland, the state automatically sends her a box containing books on how to develop her child's storytelling and reading skills. By comparison, and as we shall shortly discuss, 70% of low-income fourth-grade students in America are unable to read at a basic level.[2]

All of this is to say that traditionally, children in school are caused to generally appear to naturally follow the employment levels of their parents after school, so that a certain social stability is acquired in the operations of the society. While this was openly understood when school became universal for children, it became much less so as social changes demanded that all children be given equal opportunities in education. This hidden strategy of not educating school children in their reason was aimed at preserving a social imbalance that could no longer be openly acknowledged.

However, this ratio of 'managers to managed' shifted as we moved into the computer era, because with this new technology, the work sector required more workers with a university education. To enable this to happen, the university lowered its entrance standard, and the school lowered its exam standards, so that more children from lower socioeconomic levels could gain a university education.

To appear to assist students with poorer language skills to do better in these now lower standard examinations, and move to the university to meet this demand, the school simplified the teaching of grammar and placed less emphasis on the 3Rs. Yet, this not only intensified the general differences in student abilities, because it meant that students who were already well-raised knew what, those who were less well-raised could now not. In short, this lowered the standard of general education, placing great stress on the university level to maintain the quality of a degree.

All we have discussed above is clearly detailed in the books "The Illusion of Education" and "The Illusion of School". However, it may simply be now understood that:

School grades are strongly related to the language capability under which students were raised as infants.

This brings us to answer the first question: Why do normal children, being born with exactly the same ability for intelligence, continually produce stable differences in their school performance?

The most direct answer lies in the different environments in which they are raised, even within the same family. But the understanding psychologists have of the environment in regard to intelligence is too simple. The complexity of the environment really needs to be understood. However, to simplify this understanding here, we need to know how school really evaluates student ability and why it does not do this based on the student's ability/intelligence, as is claimed.

It took me many decades to discover the real underlying cause of the differences in student ability, but when I found it, it was so obvious that it seemed too simple to see. I may suggest to you here that all the differences in the performance of different students come down to what I call "The Art of Sensitivity in Awareness", when this is applied by parents and educators to the child and student, and when the student applies this to their learning.

Accordingly, any child, and I have been assisting students in this for many, many decades, may have their school performance and subsequent grades significantly raised, provided the parent or the educator takes the time to be sensitive to the emotional needs of the individual human student, at whatever age they may be.

Incidentally, the idea that we learn better at certain times of our life and that our learning becomes restricted as we age is totally wrong and based on a misunderstanding of the idea of critical periods, which I explain in considerable detail in "Brain Plasticity: How the Brain Learns through the Mind to create Intelligence".

You never stop learning, while the mind desires it so.

Yet, school was never to encourage this understanding of sensitivity, because school is, by its inherent purpose, a processing system, funded by society to produce a variation of ability to meet the desired capability of the work sector. By this design, students leave their education to take on different work responsibilities, whether as a doctor, an accountant, a computer engineer, a merchant, a plumber, or, as I once was, a carpenter. Although I had had many, many jobs before I turned my attention to improving education.

To begin, let me explain that rather than thinking of an inherited brain, that we understand that it is the quality of the inquiring mind to drive physical neurons of the brain into relationships and by the emotional state of the mind to orchestrate the chemistry of neurotransmitters, which accelerate or hinder to movement of signals through the brain's networks, that the student learns.

There again, if I were to explain to you (as we will come to examine) that learning is not brain ability, but of the mind continually trying to satisfy its two basic survival instincts:

- Am I safe?

- What is the most interesting thing for me at this moment?

When these are not adequately met, the student's mind drifts. When it drifts, the student loses track with what they should be learning. This sets off a host of unanswered questions and confusion. Understanding this leads us to the real cause of differences in ability, performance, and grades.

While this is explained in depth further in the book, we may understand here how wrong we are to assume that the top student has better intelligence. After all, we too often state "She's really intelligent" when we think of the girl who always gives the right answer in the right way. Equally, we also witness a teacher shouting at a student in their class, stating, "You are so stupid." In both of these, we are wrong. The estimation we have of an individual's intelligence has nothing to do with their academic learning, and so their performance in a class with all the marks and grades that come with it.

School, I discovered, and as we shall see, works on two languages. These are mathematics and the language used for normal communication in the school, be this English, Chinese, or Arabic. These languages work upon rules, a never-ending construction of rules. If the student is able to satisfy the two instincts of the mind and each of their teachers knows how to truly assist them in this, which few actually do, the student will focus upon each rule presented to them and will practice upon each to be proficient. As they gain confidence with the rules of the languages, they will see relationships more easily with the information and facts they are to learn.

As they discover these are relevant and interesting, they will develop, through their sensitivity, good memory networks. These will enable them to more readily recognise the meaning of new information by relating it to previous information and see good applications for this. By their quality of language, they will explain their mind to those evaluating their response, and by the guidance they obtain, feel inspired to be more successful.

Such would be the natural state if each student were to learn alone with a teacher, but this is not school. School is for groups of individuals having different egos, needs, and drives who are forced to learn together information that becomes increasingly more complex. As the school monitors who can keep the pace, it seeks to recognize who will be routed to university and who will not.

Through the competition this creates, students develop varying insecurities that may lead them to help others, but will more generally cause them to hinder the progress of others in their pursuit of personal recognition from the teacher, hoping this will improve their marks. As insults and intimidation are generated by this group psychology, a general feeling of inadequacy is bred within students, hampering their confidence to ask questions and hindering their means to pursue responses to gain the understanding each needs.

As insecurities play on the mind of the student, the first factor of the mind comes into play, and, **in not being safe**, they are distracted from a rule. Not sure of what they missed, they guess how to proceed, and without corrective instruction, move into a process of confusion. As understandings become a mixture of being known and unsure, each student progresses through their lessons displaying variation with all others.

The teacher notices how the response of each student varies from what they expect and marks each accordingly. They have too little time to, or understanding of, how to bring all up to their expectations, with the mark they dispense becoming a state of their mind, as to what they think each student is capable of. An evaluation that becomes reinforced in their mind in the next lesson, and those that subsequently follow this. As the teacher accepts the variations in responses of their students, so each student conforms to what is expected of them.

After all, a student who always gains 5/10 would never expect to get 10/10 and never seek to explore why they can't. They accept what they are told they are worth and seldom realise the real potential they have. This is school. It is a self-limiting environment, designed to be this way.

Withstanding this for the moment and as may have been understood from what has so far been revealed, one meaningful way to bring about the much-needed transformation of the school would be to educate all teachers and parents to understand that grades are not a consequence of effort and ability, albeit intelligence. Instead, it would be for them to be educated to understand that student performance is reliant upon the state of the student's mind, as I have explained, and be educated in ways for parents to raise and teachers to teach that stimulate the second factor of the mind by presenting information in a lively, interactive way with continual feedback and purpose.

If done correctly, students who missed part of a lesson due to distraction or boredom would have the opportunity to gain a clearer understanding and be better able to self-correct their development. Such a way would enable all students to gain higher marks. I know this to be so because I have worked towards this purpose for most of my life, and have developed a method of teaching that enables every one of 50 in a class to understand and keep up with each lesson.

We can make a real difference in the understandings our students gain, but only if we really understand how school works and the real purpose it has. To do this, we may now explore the content of the very many, many pages I lay before you.

All in all, the books I have written discuss how any student, regardless of their age, and I include adults here, can learn to improve their learning and so affect the grades that education rewards them with. They also emphasize that the identity of the school must radically change.

As we have discussed, the purpose of school is to produce potential workers of different abilities for the working world. However, as we discuss in "The Real Dangers of AI", and other books, AI is expected to take over so many jobs that the purpose of people in society must change. Too many will never work and never have the opportunity for this. AI, itself, recognizes that I am the first scientist to openly discuss how this incredibly high level of unemployment will create very high levels of depression. In turn, this will breed many societal ills: rises in alcoholism and substance abuse, family breakdowns, child neglect and abuse, and a substantial rise in organized crime. In turn, governments will counter this disharmony within their society by the use of AI in all its many forms for surveillance, policing, and security.

Basically, this is to say that the design and total operation of the school must change. No longer is it to produce citizens driven by insecurity to work, but citizens of a high moral responsibility to their society with higher levels of empathy, consideration, and tolerance than it has ever produced before. This subject is covered in other books; here, we explore how every child can learn in a safe, happy, and highly interactive environment guided by educationalists and supported by parents who understand the Art of Sensitivity in Awareness.

All in all, human beings vary in all they do, which is what makes us beautifully human, but school could become more competent if the governing factor really wanted it to be so. To date, there has been no real incentive for this from the working and social world. Rapid developments in nanotechnology and more advanced levels of artificial intelligence will create this.

Roy Andersen

The Illusion of School

by

Roy Andersen

The Illusion of School follows from the Illusion of Education, which provides a more in-depth account of how education really woks. The book you are about to read builds upon this, and offers thoughts for Parents, Educators and Students how the school really works, the illusion behind it, and how all may better gain from this understanding.

_____.

Chapter One

The Role of Education

The cornerstone of every society is its education; the ways in which the children of today are prepared to be the adults of tomorrow. The very most of us do not see this larger picture, and look upon education as the means by which our children can gain security in their lives.

So, we worry about the grades they get and the opportunities education may give them. Based on our understanding of how its systems work and the resources at our disposal, we do what we can. To those of us more able in this affair, we put into operation strategies that will guide our children through the better channels of education, in the hope that this will give them more rewarding opportunities in life. To those of us less able or less aware of the true nature of education, we convince ourselves that in our more egalitarian times, things will work out all right, and our child will stand a good chance of a good job. It all seems straightforward. Good grades equal good security.

At least, this is how it used to be, but with a global economy that brings one recession too close to the one that preceded it, and more people moving about the world for work than ever before, the chances of our child getting any job, let alone the one they desire, is not as easy as it once was. With worry, if not desperation, we turn to education and demand better service from it.

The pressure on education to improve the quality of its product is not new. Within the last century, education changed its tactics many times, endeavoring to meet the demands placed upon it by advances in technology, which required more able workers, and by social changes that sought a fairer society.

Despite these efforts of education, employers today complain of graduates who cannot write a decent letter. One teacher, we find, who has taught 6,000 high school students in his career, reflects that most students he meets today do not know how to form a sentence correctly.[3] While poor grammar and so poor language are serious problems, it is not the only ones.

A recent LEAF Survey found that a third of 16 to 23-year-olds did not know that eggs come from hens. One-tenth of these young people actually thought that eggs come from wheat.[4] In 2014, a survey by the National Science Foundation found that 26% of 2,200 people did not know the Earth revolved around the Sun. Half of these interviewed, some 48 per cent, did not know that human beings evolved from earlier species of animals, which is Darwin's basic theory of evolution.[5] When we consider all this, we are caused to take seriously the complaints of professional people about the quality of education children are receiving today.

Just as importantly, we are caused to reflect upon the kind of citizen we are producing for the future, when we come across a 2014 poll which found: "Children are living in an unprecedented toxic climate in which they skip meals to stay thin, get bombarded by porn, are bullied, and fear they will be failures amid a continuous onslaught of stress at school."[6] According to this, and other sources, half of 2,000 children and adolescents interviewed admitted they were bullied and fearful in school. Forty percent of those 2,000 children claimed their relationship with other children had been severely distorted by online pornography. Studies show that depression is now a major factor in our societies, seriously affecting children.

It seems reasonable to suggest from this that we are not teaching children, and so not preparing the future adult citizen, how to deal with the stresses and strains in their lives. Life in school today is not as we knew it in our time.

Children are not to be blamed for this. They are innocent to the world and rely upon us to fashion it for them. It was, after all, partly for this reason that a general education was brought into being. However, while the young child of today is easily competent with sophisticated software, and lives in an ever-expanding social universe that encourages their intelligence, the underlying mechanism by which they are educated, we may say processed, is much the same as it was when a general education was first set up.

Now, as then, and as we stress the point, education accepts the way the child thinks, as it processes them through its system. It does not attempt to teach the child how to think. This is the whole problem today with education. By not teaching children how to think, it relies upon their background skills to educate them. In earlier times, children were better disciplined in their social environment to the opportunities, however restricted they were, that education provided. This caused them to be more responsible to their learning, even though they were more diversified in their mental preparation for this.

However, as we have just mentioned, the schoolchild of today has far too many social difficulties to contend with, to be as simply processed by education. They need more time to understand what they need to learn and why they should want to learn this. So, while the teacher struggles under more stress to develop their students, those students are more confused than ever before as to what is happening in their lives. Therefore, while education has tried to improve itself, and in many ways it has done this, it has failed in the most important way.

We may consider that the quality of education has progressed from earlier times, and so the ability of children in school has improved accordingly. It may then be somewhat surprising to look upon a normal examination paper for 12-year-old children a hundred years ago, and wonder how the child of today would fare with it.

If I may quote from a Bullitt County school examination paper of 1912, we would find that among many other things, children of that time were expected to be able to spell: antecedent, partial and monotony. They were asked in Arithmetic to calculate how much money a man lost when he sold his watch for 180 dollars, which was 16 and two-thirds per cent of what he paid for it. In the Grammar Section, they were asked to list and define the parts of speech. In Geography, they were asked to name the waters a vessel would pass through sailing from England to Manila via the Suez Canal. History required them to sketch Sir Walter Raleigh, and in the section on Civil Government, they were asked to explain three duties of the President and define what veto power means.[7] All these questions, of course, had to be answered in very neat copperplate handwriting.

In thinking about this, I asked a 12-year-old girl today what country she would like to visit. The girl replied Portugal. I asked her if she knew where Portugal is. She replied: "It is inside Spain". I then asked her if she knew the capital of Portugal. "Brazil," She replied.

Understanding the difficulty, if not impossibility, of many children today to pass such an examination as this one of 1912, it may be argued that education today is not about the acquisition of knowledge, but about how the student can search for the information they require. However, searching for information requires that the student knows what to search for, and this makes them reliant either upon the instructions of another or upon what they know. It arises from this that the smaller their knowledge base, the more they must rely upon instruction. As this is so for the child in school, so it is for the worker and citizen in society. It is from this that we are brought to consider how education prepares the child of today to be the worker and citizen of tomorrow. Let us move now to consider what education means from the viewpoint of the child.

Before adolescence, children want the security of being loved. This, basically, is all they want, and they contrive in all manner to gain the attention of their teacher to develop a bond of security. Each child in a class will devise their own strategies to this purpose. These will range from blatant affection of the teacher, to doing something evil to another child to gain the attention of the teacher. Innocent-looking children can employ the most Machiavellian schemes to get what they want. Their problem, of course, is that they have to survive among the personalities of the other children in the class to develop their own sense of identity, while at the same time seeking the teacher's recognition of their presence. During this conflict of drives (to show compliance to the teacher and a competitive attitude to their peers), children are aware that the teacher is giving them information, but they do not really understand why.

They think the teacher wants them to be good, and they believe that to show that they are good is to give the right answer, faster than any of their competitors. In this way, children begin their education focusing on the answer, and not on how the answer could be obtained. Education, to a child, is very much a win-or-lose situation. They begin to role-play how they should interact with information in the very early stages of their school life, based upon their perception of how they rank with other children.

Since children will not normally change their class, they move through their school life with much the same peers and so demonstrate the same behavioural and intellectual performance that gives them their recognition. Good or bad, clever or not so, this is the means by which they come to know themselves in their class, and so how their mind is cultivated to learn. It is through this conditioning environment that the mind of the child is caused to recognise its ability, through what their teacher says of it. A child who is always given a mark of 6/10 will not believe or understand why they should ever gain 10/10, and so will never really analyse what they could do better. In short, the child is trained to trust the teacher's impression of their effort, rather than being trained to question that impression and so break free from the imposition placed upon their worth.

As they mature, students do not understand how to change the strategies they have created and built upon to answer questions, nor do they understand why they should. They continue to see school as a place where the teacher wants the right answer, and their purpose is to provide this by any means. Distracted by each other, they are unable to concentrate wholly on the movement of information in a lesson, and so gain only a generalized sense of its worth. So, they learn to accept information in fragments and believe this is both normal and acceptable. As lesson follows lesson, they develop their own personalised and incomplete structures of knowledge.

As they move into and through adolescence, they struggle with the natural process of developing their identity. As they begin to reject the presence of their parents, to create the space for their identity to develop, so they seek to distance themselves from the teacher for the same reason. While the child may see the teacher in the role of a parent, the older student sees them as a representative of authority who is only there to tell them what they cannot do. This, of course, is all in a generalized sense.

However, the significance now is that since the adolescent no longer seeks to impress the teacher, they have lost the purpose for which they had to give the right answer. Yet, the answer is all they have developed to focus upon, because nobody has told them why they are learning what they are learning. Students, then, copy from each other within school. Or outside of school, they play computer games and watch TV, while they scan through their textbooks seeking only to find the best answer that will earn them a better mark. Once they have found an answer, they hope to trick their teacher into believing they have methodically derived it and so understand it by padding out an explanation. However, the only thing the student is concentrating on is the mark they will gain. The lower the mark, and the more red ink on their paper, which points out the mistakes they have made, the more they will hide their work from others in their class.

This aside, as each student advances in a subject, they rely upon the broken and disrupted steps of knowledge they have acquired to demonstrate a level of competence. The strategies they have personally developed to handle information will be applied to all their subjects, so that the teacher of each will sense a generalized level of their ability.

However, if they are notably happy or more unhappy with one teacher or one subject atmosphere, their performance can change accordingly in that subject.

Yet, the student still will not have learned how to understand what they are learning. They will have committed information to memory, but very few will be able to confidently explain how they derived their answer or what it really means. Eventually, after 12 years or so in school, depending on their educational system, they take their final examinations, gain a mark somewhere between excellent to failure, and either go into higher education or (hopefully) into the job market.

However, for those who go to university, something different will happen. For the first time in their life, they will be taught how to learn to reason and how to understand how to question information. They will engage in critical thinking. Why, we may ask, and why only for these students?

While it is true that today general education tries to incorporate ideas of critical thinking into projects, this is not quite what we mean here, and we will return to explain this in greater detail later. At this moment, to understand why it is only university students who are taught to think better, we need to understand the purposes of education. Traditionally, we see these as being threefold:

1) It is to take unruly and undisciplined minds, and turn these into conditioned individuals able to behave socially and morally, as their society requires of them.

2) It is to teach them skills of reading, writing, arithmetic, and general awareness, so they can learn to be competent in a job purpose. However, as the required ability for jobs varies, so education is required to provide students of different

capabilities. It achieves this by processing the reasoning skills and the aptitude of the student (which are really decided by their home/parental influences), and the ability to overcome distraction to manifest their work potential.

3) It is to divide its product between those who are to complete only their general education, and those who will go on to a higher and specifically a university education. In the case of the former, these are regarded to become the managed citizens who will be directed to worker responsibility in their society. They are not regarded to be taught how to reason beyond the individual skills they were raised in by their parents. Those of the latter are destined to take the place of managers in government and business. They are taught skills of reason to enable them to be more competent in the more serious tasks they will undertake in their society. However, as technology changes, so it requires education to change the proportions of who should be taught higher reasoning skills.

To the people of the 19th century and for most of the 20th, these factors were well recognized. However, today these requirements of education have become slightly obscure through the social changes that arose out of the 1960s and 70s.[8] They also became less tenable as the general intelligence rose to new levels through the technological influences that began shortly after this. It is much because of the greater equality of our times that we have forgotten what the real purposes of education are. While its first requirement is obvious, the second and third require some introduction here.

A society functions through different job skills, with each skill requiring its own level of competence. It is the purpose of education to provide a variety of abilities to match the competence that each skill area requires.

When the technological level is reasonably constant, as it was in the late agricultural stage, it was relatively easy for education to provide the upcoming generation with the same capability for the jobs that had been done by their parents. At that time, employment had a sense of inheritance, where the son would be skilled in thinking by his father and move into his father's profession. In a generalized sense, opportunity in education worked to support this, so that a doctor's son became a doctor and a blacksmith's son a blacksmith. It was through this inheritance of occupation that family names had been earlier decided, and by this designation, a family was socially classified in their society.

Accordingly, it was easy for education to achieve the variation of competence expected of it by relying upon the thinking skills the child had incorporated from the job skills of their father, and through the social influences that contained the ways their family saw and interacted with their world. As each child entered into education, school taught them reading, writing, and general knowledge, and used these home-based skills of thinking and the aptitude each had evolved through to direct them to a sphere of employment.

- We need to realise here how the greater mass of people in the industrial era lived through "a trance of routine," because we have forgotten this today. The people who worked in mills and factories lived with jobs that were routine. Their minds were not stimulated in the work they did, and too often they were exhausted after work to think upon the world. It was with this mental conditioning that they raised their children, and so were caused to make intelligence socially inherited.

There was at that time, we may realise, no need and no requirement to teach children how to think better than they had been conditioned to do through their home and social environment. In fact, to incorporate into the curriculum of the 19th century a subject, or part of one that taught children how to reason better, would not only have been unnecessarily expensive, but it would have been regarded to seed further disharmony into a social structure that was nervously facing anarchy at that time. Knowledge, after all, is control, so that from the point of view of its government, the danger with education was always the fear that it could raise ability faster than it could be controlled.

The one and truly effective policy that gave education and society complete control over this balance was the propagated belief that the child could only be as good as their parents. It is the legacy of this inherited ability that underlies exactly the problems education has today and will much more come to have in the future. It is for this reason that much of our discussion revolves around this issue.

Throughout the industrial era and up until the computer era, this "family to work" routing process worked adequately well for education. However, as we moved towards the end of the 20th century and became IT-oriented, greater demand began to be placed upon education to produce workers more able to match the new job skills that were beginning to surface. We are led from this to begin to examine how, and to begin to understand why, education has managed its control of intelligence so well for so long.

Some noted individuals in the past have striven to create policies and practices to make the educational experience happy and meaningful for the child. John Dewey and Maria Montessori are two famous names from many who come to mind. Indeed, education is filled with good teachers who endeavour to create the educational dream. Most, however, eventually succumb to the pressures of their system and resign themselves to what education is really about.

Concealed behind the scenery of a caring institution, which its employees earnestly commit themselves to, is the simple and basic plan of the educational machine. This is to monitor the ability of each student to deal with the tasks with which it confronts them. To decipher the quality of each student, education defined intelligence as a largely innate process. This enabled it to refine, but not alter, the skills of reason that each child uses in its system. By this means, the student was cheaply and efficiently processed from an unruly and undisciplined child to the grade of potential worker their society required them to be.

As each society functions, it requires x members to operate in the managerial and professional classes, y members to operate in the skilled class, and z members to perform the host of ancillary tasks that support these two. It is the function of education to provide workers who are generally competent to meet the demands of each of these categories, to allow the work and so the social system to function as effectively as possible.

As a machine of operation, education is not interested in children developing their ability beyond that with which they began school. Those who run the system don't have the money for this. Besides, most educationalists were raised, and so educated themselves, to be unaware of what this could mean. Most believe it would not do any good, because they believe the child's intelligence was more or less decided the moment they were conceived. School is merely a processing system, as a part of a processing society, controlled by economists who operate on a cost-conscious basis, governed strictly by political control. One only has to confer with a school administrator upon the restrictions of their budget to see where the limitations in the progressiveness of education are found accountable.

As an educational system seeks to coordinate teaching standards and assessment levels on a national basis, it determines acceptable levels of performance and regulates teachers to provide variations in their assessments of these levels. As the average level is decided, and as teachers are caused to set their marks upon this, so a few students in each class gain high marks, a few low marks, and most gain marks about the average. In an ideal world, this average is set to a level that is believed to match the normal operational capability for the working requirements of the society at that time.

As children engage in their learning, they adapt their own particular systems of dealing with information to the rules education uses to define the level of this average. By the effectiveness of their personal systems to think, the effort they give, and the ability they have to overcome the distractions that seek to interfere with these, each child presents a profile of their ability. Education sets this profile about the point of average, so that all children can be seen to vary about this as it is expected of them.

Unaware of the means of allocation to which they are subject, children fail to understand why their efforts are not greatly rewarded, for if one child should rise in their performance, another would inevitably fall. All of this is because, in a generalized sense, children compete for place marks about the average that is set by the teacher, and which was set for them by the educational system.

Education is able to work like this because it regards the intelligence of the child to be generally fixed (or inherited). This reasoning enables the teacher to observe the effort of the student as they progress through their lessons, and allows them to use the marks they award as evidence of the potential of the student. In this way, education simply matches the capability of its students to the required capability for jobs in its society, as each student is dispatched to a designated area of employment. This mechanical operation of education has not changed since the time of John Dewey a hundred years ago. As he wrote at that time:

"We welcome a procedure, which under the title of science sinks the individual in a numerical class, judges him with reference to capacity to fit into a limited number of vocations ranked according to present business standards, assigns him to a pre-destined niche and thereby does whatever education can do to perpetuate the present order..."[9]

The whole operation of education is, therefore, set about the concept of averages. It is for this reason that teachers are conditioned to regulate the grades they give about the midpoint of the average. Should a teacher allow the average score they present to their system to fall too far below this mark, a question is raised about their competence. If they raise the average level too far above this, suspicion arises as to how this could be done, for it places pressure upon other teachers as to why they have not achieved this, and embarrassment on the system for failing to set the correct mark for the average. By such effort, the teacher places themselves in a precarious position, from which all are waiting for them to fall.

Most teachers, it is too little realized, live in a world where they are drained by administrative tasks, and exhausted in trying to patch up the inadequate thinking and behavioural skills on which parents and society have raised their students. With too little resource to attend to the questions, four or five are waiting to ask, while they struggle to explain to one child what they do not understand, and know there are ten or more who don't know how to ask the question, the teacher can only throw seeds in the air and see where they land. It is just too easy for the teacher to concede defeat, take the average given to them, and set the score of their students around this. At the end of the day, who would really notice the difference?

When a concerned parent challenges a teacher, they seek excuse in the natural ability of the child or the system under which they operate. Yet, if another teacher of a different personality replaces that teacher, and who uses different tactics, the child can suddenly see things they never could before, gain better results, and become "more" intelligent. Their new profile merges with the events of their life, and they become accepted for who they are now. Their earlier image, if not forgotten, is excused in the most blameworthy factor, which tends to be the teacher. So when things go wrong, the parents blame the teacher, and the teacher blames the child. Education can too easily become a cesspit, where everyone is blaming everyone else, and all the child wants to do is to go and play.

The teacher, however, is no less a human being than the child; each has their own desires, needs, happiness, and problems. The problems for teachers today are not as simple as they once were; now they are burdened with increasing administrative tasks that sap the energy they should reserve for teaching.

Teachers have always had to learn how to control disordered children, for the task of education is to change free minds into minds that will conform. However, now they have to learn how to control students who are more abusive and violent than ever before.

It is the teachers who are the ones who deal with the problems caused by society managers on a daily basis, and often receive little gratitude for it. They are told how to improve their ways of teaching for children to do better, but are seldom given the resources to do so. Too often, a huge gulf exists between psychologists who debate about learning and developmental tactics on paper and then send these papers to teachers who try to make their ideas work with 40 screaming kids in the space of 45 minutes.

- By the conditioning of their training and the circumstances under which they operate, teachers, despite their personal views, are caused to see child performance as too much a part of some inborn quality, to understand how learning strategies and skills of reason evolve to create what they understand the child's intelligence to be.

In consequence to this, few teachers are aware of the importance for their students to control the rate of knowledge they are absorbing, in progression with their own values of association. Yet, it is precisely this that provides information with the relevance of higher transfer ability, so that the learner can better understand. This, after all, is the means that enables them to have greater accuracy and faster processing skills in the ways they recognise and solve problems.

Teachers may argue otherwise and say that their students do understand them, though seldom do they engineer efficient feedback systems that would ensure this. The problem here is not in the effort or the capability of the teacher, but in the ways they have been trained to understand the capability of their students, and the systems they move through as they endeavour to prepare them for jobs after school. All who are in this machine, headmasters, teachers, children, and their parents, struggle against the design of education to give children a fairer and greater opportunity in life.

Despite these efforts, most children, if not virtually all, see school as a place they never understand. It is a strange world that seems alien to all the values they hold. As years pass, each child develops survival tactics that allow them to be accepted by other children, and cause them to behave in their learning by what they think, the teacher thinks, is relevant. The work they are given is seldom understood, and even when it is it holds little relevance. The little that makes sense in each new lesson is added to all the parts that went before that did not. Through the world they came from, and how they are able to settle into this world of school, each child phases into their own familiarity with the contents of their lessons. Some children become smarter in learning how to play the academic rules, while others become less so. Those who do, gain high marks; those who don't, fail. Ever wary of what others think of them, children learn to hide their failures, pretend to understand when they don't, and resign themselves to the grade they get, believing it to be an inevitable evaluation of their worth. They, like we before them, are conditioned to this.

It is to be realized that the philosophies that guide students in their learning are designed for individuals to learn through group experience. In their normal education, students do not develop through corrective and individualistic feedback. Instead, they strive to make sense of their lessons through their home-based ideas of how to think. This is said to be their intelligence, but really it is only the strategies they have acquired that enable them to evaluate the possibilities they recognise.

In a simple sense, this lies in their effort to search for information that is not obvious, how they select a goal and subgoals, how they identify errors, and so how they monitor the overall progression of information. All these factors are very decisive to performance. They are all developmental, and none of them relies upon a genetic quality for their efficiency. That one child might be faster and another slower, one more able to recognise parts another cannot, and know how to test a hypothesis while the other looks blank, have all been shown to lie in developmental and correctable processes.[10] How, then, does education view how its students are placed in their learning?

Chapter Two

The Bell Curve

When the competence of one is compared to that of another, there must be some difference. In a class of children, these differences will normally be set about an average. Therefore, the calculations to understand the ability of children in education, and so any predictions made of their expected use to society, will be based on the concept of averages. Any discussion and use of an average, and the extent of its extremities (the higher and lower values), will be projected through a very particular graph that is rooted in projections of intelligence.

This graph has acquired three labels in its history. It was first called *"The Gauss Curve,"* then *"The Standard Distribution Curve,"* and finally *"The Bell Curve"* — because of its shape. This graph is widely used in statistics, but when it is used to explain the ability, albeit intelligence, of children, and so any aspect of them in education or society, it is said to project a mixture of their inborn or inherited worth and how they have so far developed. Such a graph describes how the number of children, or people in a population, who were tested (as set upon the y axis), can be related to their test scores (set along the x axis) to show how their intelligences vary.

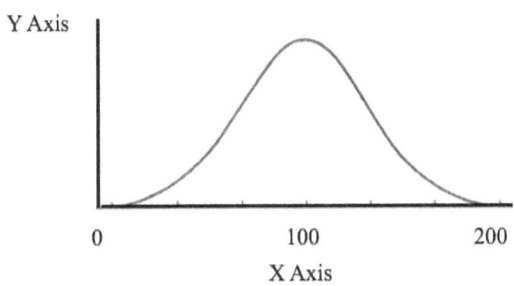

This graph will play a small role in our discussions in this book, but it will be greatly discussed and play a very major role in our following book, "Intelligence: The Great Lie." For this reason, it is important that we gain some simple understanding of it here. The first thing we should realize is that this graph is merely the outline shape of a number of divisions.

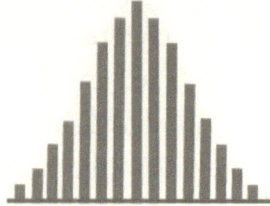

Each division/column represents the scores of a number of individuals, with the height of each column telling us how many obtained that score. We can see in the diagram above how the majority of individuals obtained average scores, while a lesser number obtained progressively higher and lower scores on either side of this average. We can visualize from this how 'theoretically' scores range from zero on the left to a maximum of 200 on the right, with a score of 100 being taken as the average value of intelligence.

This would be to say that scores on the extreme right indicate supreme intelligence in the individual. This is where we would expect to find Einstein, for example. While on the extreme left, we would find individuals with extreme learning problems, such as an individual with Down Syndrome. All other individuals are said to vary between these two extremes, with the intelligence of the average individual given a score of 100.

As politicians plan how the next generation of workers can be matched to the predicted needs of their time (they plan too little ahead), they create policies that open doors for some children and close them to others in their social and educational development. They do this based upon the advice they gain from psychologists, as to whether the gene is more responsible for intelligence or if the environment is.

Some believe that, as a rule of thumb, children from wealthier parents would naturally score more than 100 in an IQ test, while children from poorer parents would naturally score less than 100. Yet, it is totally wrong to consider that any such group ranking, where it is shown to occur, is brought about by natural or rather inherited inheritance.

In our following book, "Intelligence: The Great Lie" we shall discuss that in 1994, a book, aptly named *"The Bell Curve,"* tried to make an argument that African Americans and Hispanics in America have low-quality genes for intelligence. Its authors used this argument to raise the issue that money should not be wasted on their education and social-related programs, trying to do what nature cannot by giving these people better educational opportunities.[11] Their book was based on 'manufactured lies' according to a leading psychologist. In 2013, a paper was put forward in British education under a conservative government,[12] similarly arguing that intelligence is largely determined by inheritance. The paper recommended that schools serving 'better' areas should be given more money to improve the opportunities of children having greater natural ability, for the good of society.

We see in this a general tendency for right-wing factions in a society to argue that inheritance is very decisive in the child's intelligence, as a means to maintain the status quo in the next generation. The timeless argument used to support this is that successful people living in better areas are only so because they inherited high-quality genes, which they passed on to their children.

In contrast, left-wing factions argue that the environment is more important than the quality of genes inherited, as they seek to protect the interests of poorer children. From their point of view, they see success as being based on opportunity and connections, realizing that education creates these opportunities. So, they demand free and equal opportunity in education, especially at the university level.

Realizing too well that passage through university is what really decides who will do what in society, the right-wing faction seeks to control this opportunity. They attempt to do this in a number of ways. More openly, they insist that the university level should be privately funded, to reduce the chance of poorer parents being able to afford this education for their child. In less obvious ways, they instigate social programs that subtly hinder the development of children from left-wing backgrounds, as we shall come to discover. In some countries, these policies of education are very open; in others, they are very discreet. But in all countries, it is the trust placed on the impressions of intelligence gained from the graph called The Bell Curve that decides the success of any policy.

We should now be aware that the belief that genetic differences in the whole population cause differences in their intelligence is not proven.

It is, in fact, only a theory based on the observation that a tiny fraction of the population has some known distinguishable inability related to inheritance, such as a chromosomal mutation causing Down Syndrome, or, for that matter, incurred some pre-birth complications, such as oxygen starvation. All these conditions produce visible signs in the human child that cause them to differ in some way from children normally born.

What is missed in this argument is that such genes cannot be predicted. They may or may not appear in the next generation, or perhaps in some future generation, or they may never appear again. Human genetics is an unpredictable lottery, with no stability that provides any prediction of occurrence. More simply, it cannot be known or calculated which genes will appear when the child is conceived.

However, despite differences in their physiology, their existence as human beings is wrongly used to illustrate how the intelligence of the entire population is based on the genes they inherited, and which can be developed to some extent through environmental experiences.

However, this argument does not hold water, because if we go to the extreme right of the curve, we would find those who have a genius quality of intelligence. We may think of Newton, or Einstein, or Steven Hawking, by example. The significance here is that no genius ever came from a genetic line of geniuses, and never created a line of geniuses. The ancestors and descendants of every genius were quite ordinary people and not distinguished in any way. Therefore, the supreme quality of intelligence a genius has has no genetic base.

Therefore, if those who inherit or have created some distinguishable characteristics before birth, which cause them to be mentally less capable than the normal child and there is no evidence that inheritance explains geniuses, then we should consider the genius and the child who is also normally born to develop their intelligences from genes that do not differ in their quality and merely provide the human being with the ability to have intelligence.

This is also true for many genes that enable the feature to develop in a changing environment, such as language. We all inherit the same gene coding for intelligence, and we all develop this skill solely through exposure. That is, with the exception of children born with differences affecting their sensory systems, as we mentioned above. In knowing this, it is of no small consideration to realise that the root from which intelligence develops is language!

To consider the plausibility of what I suggest here, it would be illustrative to learn how the whole idea of an inherited intelligence came about and how the idea arose that it can be measured.

Psychologists like to state that Professor Binét in France in 1905, was the first to measure intelligence, as a way to give credibility to their science. This is not accurate, as I will shortly explain. The idea to measure intelligence began in a very, very different way.

In 1848, every country on the continent was rocked by revolutions. The establishment was terrified, and although these revolutions were put down with bloodshed, socialism began to grow in the lower classes. For 2,000 years, the established order had been maintained by subjugation, intimidation, and military force. However, the rise of intellectualism at this time cautioned the use of such force, and some subtle means were sought to maintain the existing hierarchy under a monarchical state.

It was a cousin of Charles Darwin who came up with the idea that every feature and function of a family line is naturally passed to its children. This is to say that as the child inherited the recognizable chin or nose of their parents, they also inherited their brains and how clever this was. This cleverness was to be measured by the work and social achievement of the family line.

Most simply, the presence of a facial feature in a royal child, similar to that in the king, was said to give evidence that the child had also inherited the natural ability to rule, because the king and his ancestors had always ruled. The same principle applied to sons of lawyers, accountants, merchants, labourers, and farmhands. From the top to the very bottom of the social system, each was to have the ability that their ancestors had demonstrated.

At this time, in 1869, neither genes nor brain cells had been discovered. In fact, the brain was looked upon as any other organ of the body. It simply worked, as it worked. So, this idea was readily grabbed by the establishment and was sent out to the public at large to create a belief that you could never be better than you are, and to respect your betters. It was the ideal means to 'keep everyone in their place'.

Events moved on, and a problem arose within the French army. France had lost the 1871 war against Prussia, and as the new century began, the French military staff were trying to improve the abilities of the common soldier in expectation of another war with Germany. Indeed, this was to come, but one of the problems the school system had, which ultimately supplied men to be soldiers, was the difficulty of knowing if a child who struggled to learn did so because of an organic problem or because they were raised under poor environmental conditions.

Binét was employed to solve this problem, which he did with the help of Théodore Simon. Together they designed a one-to-one verbal examination based on the mental age of the child to the age they could perform at in tests.

Binét was very strict to point out that intelligence can never be measured and his test was never to be used for this purpose.

However, an American psychologist by the name of Goodard discovered Binéts test while on holiday in Europe. He took it back to the States, corrupted the design, and created a simple intelligence test. At that time, the American immigration system was struggling with something like 5,000 hopeful immigrants a day, which it could not handle. Goodard was given the task of rejecting potential immigrants of undesired backgrounds at that time, Jews, Slavs, whoever it happened to be. Goodard set his intelligence test with questions about culture, which if people failed, they were returned to Europe.

This was the first time so-called intelligence tests came into public notice. Shortly after, a psychologist by the name of Terman reformed Binéts one-to-one verbal test into a sheet of tic box questions, so that thousands of people could take the test at the same time, and after an hour of answering, have their intelligence graded for life.

Terman then, by how he selected the questions, measured the intelligence of Hispanics and African Americans, and produced results to show that these people had less intelligence than white 'protestants', and should be excluded from working in all forms of government. So, a lengthy story goes on.

All we need to note here is that psychologists have ever since argued between themselves as to whether it is inheritance or the environment that is more responsible for the intelligence of an individual.. We have understood the politics behind this. In fact, there is still no agreed-upon definition of what intelligence is. So, while psychologists direct educators on how children learn and should be evaluated with grades to know their intelligence for a work role, they still do not know what intelligence actually is.

Long after the Science of Psychology had been embedded in public and governmental interests, the Science of Genetics began. Johannsen, who discovered the effect of the environment on the gene, argued that the word 'inheritance' should never be used in genetics. Half a century later, the science of neurology slowly began to understand how the brain works. With the very recent discovery that new brain cells grow, neurologists began to understand what the term Brain Plasticity could mean. Yet, cognitive psychologists, whose existence depends upon the belief that intelligence is inherited, keep their thoughts to themselves and continue to gain prestige, fame, and a lot of money selling the idea that intelligence is measurable.

Many rightwing psychologists may like to argue that the environment has no real influence on the efficiency of the gene codes inherited. In fact, a well-known psychologist once argued that inheritance accounted for 80% of a person's intelligence.

However, because of evidence in genetics, they are forced to acknowledge that environmental experience does affect the efficiency of the gene codes inherited. This takes us back to the bell curve graph.

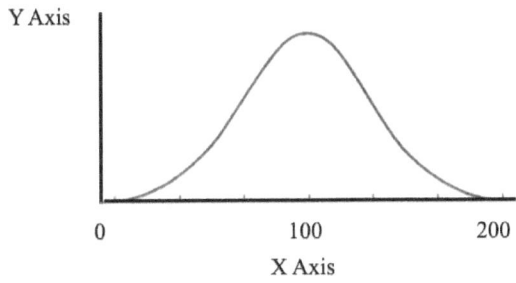

Psychologists use this graph to explain how the efficiency of gene codes varies in a population. So, an individual's IQ score (made up of the efficiency of the genes they inherited plus the experiences they have had) places them somewhere on the x-axis.

But, as we have mentioned, it is impossible to ever know the environmental experience of an individual. Therefore, their intelligence cannot be measured. So any IQ score is meaningless, because the value of the genes is not being measured. All that is being measured is their perception of the environmental experiences they have had since birth. This appears stable, but only because most individuals remain in the same stable environment. Change the environment enough, and their IQ scores will change. Allow me to expand upon this, to show what really happens.

Psychologists use this graph to explain their reasoning, and not those of geneticists, that gene codes vary in efficiency from zero to 200. But this is pure conjecture. No-one has or can measure the gene codes for intelligence, because we do not know what they are, although we do know their effects overlap. The idea that they range from zero to 200 was created by Terman in 1917, when genetics was in its infancy. These are just numbers he created out of his head.

Yet, the reasoning is that anyone with an IQ score of 200 will be a genius, because they inherited genes of this quality, plus or minus the experiences of life they have had. But as we saw, all geniuses only inherited normal efficiency genes. Therefore, their ranking gives no indication of the efficiency of their genes. Equally, there cannot be a zero IQ score based on gene efficiency, otherwise the genes would have created a mental vegetable. However, children in Romania with normal gene efficiency were found to be living vegetables, purely because they had been totally deprived of love and attention, or rather, environmental experience. So, there is no evidence that genes are responsible for the positioning of individuals on the bell curve graph.

However, if genes do not determine how intelligent a person will be, but instead are designed to let a person's intelligence be completely shaped by their environment, as seen in the cases of the Romanian children (we shall discuss in Ch.5), then the wide range of intelligence differences shown in the bell curve could be entirely the result of life experiences.

Suppose, for example, we had a hypothetical class of students all with the same gene coding, the language development of each (being totally formed only through experience) would have inspired different interests and desires. In turn, this would have led them to engage in vastly different intellectual and behavioural experiences. As each would see any test question through their own perspective of experiences, the grades of each would vary. When set on the bell curve graph, these grades would show the same variation that is said to be caused by genetic differences -- when there were no genetic differences.

Quite simply, human beings vary in their abilities through a multitude of reasons, drive, energy, effort, boredom, distractions, etc., etc., and while these appear to be stable, they are so because the environment in which they live is stable.

The problem we have with the bell curve graph is that the way it has been very politically used in the past, as it still is today, does not open minds to the possible extent of what development in ability could mean, and so the real causes of why one child struggles to understand something another grasps instantly in school.

The idea of an inherited intelligence too much simplifies what in reality is a very complex genetic process, which geneticists still do not fully understand. Accordingly, while we evaluate a child's development on their socio-economic background, we much distort the true value of the environment that determines how their mind interacts with information.

If you understand what I explain here, all this seems a meaningless exercise. However, very few people know what I share with you. So, the mass of humanity raised on the mindset psychologists have created, support polices that affect the lives of children based on political polices given direction by IQ scores.

If you find this topic interesting, you may wish to read **"Intelligence: The Great Lie"**, said by the dean of an American university to be one of the most important books published this century.

I wrote the book in an easy language so that parents and those who know English as a second language could understand how I uncovered how the whole history of psychometric testing was built up through deliberate falsification of data, fraud, and lies by leading psychologists, as they sought to influence political decisions according to the 'evidence' they produced.

Amongst other things, the book explains why it is totally impossible to measure human intelligence, simply because we can never know the specific environment that affected the individual's thinking processes. It is too unfathomable ever to be known. Therefore, the IQ test is a complete fallacy.

As we move through this book and come to understand why the genes we inherit for intelligence do not normally influence how it develops, and that all development occurs through the complexity of the environment, the reader is taken to our following book to understand how intelligence actually becomes constructed.

Accordingly, in "Brian Plasticity: How the Brain Learns Through the Mind to Create Intelligence", we examine how the emotional sensitivity of the mind not only drives neurons in how they construct networks of understanding, but it also orchestrates brain chemistry to either accelerate or hinder the passage of signals through these. Understanding this takes us back to "The Art of Sensitivity in Awareness", which we mentioned in the Introduction.

To conclude this chapter, would be to say that 'any' test score gives no indication as to whether the student has been generally happy or sad in their life. To know of this is of no small consideration, for it is the sense of well-being an individual has that inspires or detracts them from sensitivity to explore and process information.

Nor do test scores explain whether or not the individual has been generally encouraged or discouraged by those they have lived through, just as they give no indication of the extent to which they have been bullied or abused, or currently feel secure and safe. Knowing these would give some indication of the individual's ability to focus on the development of their learning as one point is overtaken by another, and so how they may understand fully that which they are evaluated upon.

These simple factors. we mention here, are the real hidden determinants behind what we shall come to understand are a chain of acts of performance, which we perceive in a unified sense to represent the intelligence of the individual.

It is precisely because this aspect of the environment is not fully understood that there is a general tendency to explain intelligence as a part of something unknown that is inherited and then further developed with too little, if any, consideration to what this factor of development really means.

All of which introduces us to a realization that the environmental factor of a child's intelligence is made up of very many complex and indefinable factors that range from diet to emotional strategies. To be aware of these factors will be very important to us, because it is these that create the long-term stability by which the individual processed and so continues to process information to gain the score they do in 'any' test. Yet, it is only by their very absence, and indeed an ignorance of their existence, that a child's stability with intelligence can be said to be caused by their genetic competence.

Unfortunately, when we raise our children or teachers teach them in school, too little thought is placed on brain plasticity, and so how the brain of the child or the student grows and forms itself through the ways information is selected and processed. If we were more aware of the "Art of Sensitivity in Awareness," as we will discuss again, we would improve their ability to interact with the world about them, in and outside of school.

However, instead of this, we focus only on the regularity by which children appear to perform in school. So, we readily accept the regular quality of performance of a student in maths and science and so on, without reflecting too much on how they trundle through their education in a very stabilizing environment, where not very much changes in their life from the day they first entered school. Their performance, the placing they are given in class, ability, and so the impression held of their intelligence or marks, grades, etc., is all highly stable. In the 14 books I have so far written about education, we examine the real causes of this stability to explain why any normally born child can gain the highest grades, if they desire it.

Gradually, we will unravel more of how education works, but for the moment let us try to understand a little more of why school does not manage better the education of its students by understanding the worries of the mother in our next chapter and the problems she faces with her child in school, as an example of those faced by all parents and their children.

Chapter Three

The Scheme of Things

*"That you may understand what he learns,
and the way he understands it."*
Kierkegaard

"My son is dyslexic," she told me, "and the school won't do anything about it."

"Why not?" I asked.

"They said they tested him, and there was nothing wrong. But he can't read. I mean, he scans sentences and doesn't see the words. He can't learn anything. His mind works differently. But, they don't agree."

"Well! You know," I suggested, "dyslexia can be caused by problems in life."

She didn't seem to hear me, and continued in her own mind. "It's wired differently, and they won't help him. He's at the bottom of his class, and he has exams soon."

"Did you have any problems with your husband when your son was younger?"

"He's a very violent man, she replied. "We don't have anything to do with him now." She held her thoughts for a moment. "He's been bullied a lot. Other kids are always picking on him."

"Maybe the problem is not his brain, but his heart." I offered the thought. "People tell your son to read this and write that, but inside he may be lonely, hurt, and lost. He scans, because he lost the meaning to take care a long time ago. There again, if he is worried about other children, his mind will be all over the place."

The mother turned to look at me. "Do you think so?" She inquired.

Let me explain why I do ....

We see in the conversation how the mother worries about the poor performance of her son in school. The psychologists, we may understand, had tested her son and declared he is not dyslexic, while the teachers responsible for his education and in seeing his ability to be restricted believe he is. We may understand from this the frustration of the mother, for it seems that neither the teachers nor the psychologists are, for whatever reason, able to correct or significantly restructure the way the boy's mind works with information, or that they do not have the resources to create this opportunity. All parties, we may imagine, will show concern, but it appears very little will be done to change the boy's situation. The mother is not wealthy, the school is in a depressed economic area, and its educational service works to a limited budget.

The basic problem here lies in the confusion as to how much or how little the genes can be known to be responsible for the boy's performance. This is much because when we look at the performance of another, we tend to believe that the worth of the genes they inherited underlie the development we witness -- although we are never quite sure by how much!

However, within education and in the classroom, this uncertainty becomes less so as teachers notice a certain regularity in the quality of work each student gives to them. Student A will always seem to make fewer mistakes than Student B, and so will always gain a higher mark. Confronted as they are with such differences in ability, teachers will generally come to see these differences as the result of circumstances, effort, and natural ability. Since circumstances are seen to easily fluctuate, the long-term stability they have observed in a student's performance will be taken to be largely the result of a factor of inheritance. This will be especially the case with children who stand out as being slower or are seen to struggle more to understand what is happening. As the teachers noted the difficulty of this mother's boy to develop, so they referred him to psychologists to try to understand what could be done to improve his development.

The psychologists appear to believe that he is not dyslexic, at least not in an organic sense. If we assume they are correct, for we will examine similar cases where the learning difficulty of a child was said to have some genetic restriction but was found not to be so, then we may understand that his mother created her reasoning that her son's mind "works differently" and that "he scans sentences and doesn't see the words" as a way of justifying his low performance. As she has come to realise too late how her son has fallen behind in his education, she is desperate to know what to do.

We, in our turn, may well imagine what the future could be for this boy as a later citizen in his society, especially since his generation is likely to face far more social complexities than ours. Indeed, we may have little doubt that the forces unravelling in this new century will bring many changes to the ways in which people live and work and the difficulties they will struggle against.

As our account unfolds, we will understand how a society creates various social and educational strategies to engineer the development of children from different backgrounds for the working roles they will later play. Once we understand what this meant in the past and what the legacy of this means today, so it will become clear why this mother did not know what she had to do to help her son, and why she was therefore caused to be reliant upon "a system" that equally did not know how to help him. For reasons we shall explain, education, as an operational system, is deeply bathed in the belief that the child enters into it with a "family" quality of intelligence. From this point of view, education sees its responsibility as being only to feed each child with as much information as they appear to be able to understand.

We may conjure up an image of what this means by visualizing each student to have a brain resembling an empty jug with a teacher pouring water into that of each student, which they may only fill according to the different capacities of each one. In earlier times, this image would have been readily accepted by most educationalists, but today, few would be eager to agree with this because of our greater awareness of socio-economic issues. Yet, it is important for us to understand that, in having said this, the idea of each student being born with their own particular limitation to learn would lie in the back of a teacher's mind when one student understands them immediately and another appears to struggle to make sense of the same question asked.

To grasp some early awareness of what we will come to discuss in some depth, it is necessary to realise that when education came into being, it had two purposes. The first was to take the undisciplined ways of children and turn them into morally responsible citizens. The second was to fashion their disorganized minds to a level of competence, so they may later function in their society largely as their forefathers had done before them, and so maintain a sense of work opportunity and social responsibility. In this time of the agricultural era, the society operated upon a highly structured social framework, and children were largely kept to this for the later roles they could play in their society. We can still witness this social strategy in many technologically underdeveloped countries today.

However, as our technology advanced and we moved further into the industrial era and so into that of a factory mentality, so the purpose of education came to be to educate the child in school to take either a manager or a managed role in society. How the school operated to manage this and how it worked in conjunction with social programs to achieve this are important factors we need to discuss in-depth, because our school systems globally still work on this design, much to the ignorance of many educationalists today.

In time, we shall come to understand more of all this, but we may realise here that it was only through accepting the child's ability as largely inherited that school could justify cramming 50 to 80 and sometimes 100 children into a single classroom to be given instruction by a single teacher. Without this reasoning, school could never have been economically possible in its beginnings.

However, from this mindset of an inherited ability came the reasoning that students should learn through repetition, which created the mould for the style of a teacher who would be there to provide their students with knowledge and be there to correct minor mis-understandings, but by the size of their class and the conditions under which they worked teachers were never to have the time or resources to teach more effectively. In short, students were largely to be left to learn by their own devices, which of course had a socio-economic as well as a political side to it, and so were judged on what was essentially thought to be "their" ability.

Accordingly, in this scheme of things, students were to be left to learn largely in school through their home and social influences, and so the knowledge, acquired skills, and circumstances of their parents made their sense of learning. Parents, of course, could not know the subject matter of a lesson nor could they be present in the class to protect their child from the distracting influences of other children, but it is they who were to be responsible for the way their child develops to intellectually and behaviorally interact with the world.

Risely and Hart demonstrated this in how "academically" minded parents were found to have raised their children to have some 30 million words more in their vocabulary by about the age of three to four, than children of less educated parents.[13] The significance of this is not in the astonishing number of words that seem to differentiate the ability of these children, but in the ways the minds of those children of better-educated parents became better prepared for the world of school.

Accordingly, they will have been developed with a greater mental stamina to keep focused on the movement of information and so be less easily distracted, be more in tune to the manner by which one rule builds upon another to make sense and order of information, and will be more confident to inquire and so take a greater self control of their learning experience, which children otherwise raised are unlikely too have. Go into any kindergarten class and you will soon understand the importance of this early preparation, and so how such children display a higher performance on day one, which they seldom lose. Essentially, then, such better-raised children will have a far higher competence in language skills, and this we shall come to see is too often the deciding factor in the marks and grades education will award to them, and so all that will follow from this later in life.

So, we find that students who understood their lessons better and succeeded in school did so largely because their parents knew how to play the game, had prepared their children for school, and better guided them through it. For those children not so fortunate, and this would be the vast majority, who struggled in their learning or failed to understand their lessons, education excused its inefficiency by blaming the inefficiency of the social system that supported its operations.

When the socio-economic background of the child could not be blamed, education was able to defend its teachers, when they were unable to educate all their students to the parents' expectations, by blaming the biology of the child, the value of intelligence they were assumed to have inherited.

In this, nothing has changed since school began. Teachers still regularly award marks from 4/10 to 10/10 to their students without being thought to be individually responsible for the marks they give. It is to escape any irresponsibility they may be blamed for, that teachers very seldom give marks lower than 4/10. After all, if the student was marked 1/10, the question would be brought to the competence of the teacher. So, the school system tumbles on as it always has, blaming everything except itself for the vast majority of children who fail its system after 12 years of education. The truth of the matter is two-fold.

Within the school system, educators were and still are not trained to know how the mind and the brain of the student works to learn, and those who contemplate upon this are kept too busy and often exhausted by tight work schedules and disruptive classes to be able to inspire, explain and develop the learning of all of their students. As we will examine in great depth through the books of this series, the real reasoning behind this is not the apparent inefficiency of the school as it appears, but the social design placed upon the school to actually teach children how not to learn too much.

As we have just indicated, the school system globally still works on a 19th-century political ideology to process students through its system largely on their language ability and home influences to either go to university or not to do so.

The distinction is far more important than we may imagine. School children are largely raised to respect authority and not to question it, for the later compliant citizen they will be in society. They are taught to think in terms of "yes" and "no" (We will discuss why the education of critical thinking is largely ineffective later.), for the managed role they will take in the work society. So, they are taught to learn information much less than to understand why they are learning it. Hence, we teach school children what to learn but not how to learn. However, those students who manage to get into university, generally in accord with their higher language ability and better financial means, will be educated in higher reasoning skills for the managers in society and industry they are to be.

This stratification is very deliberate. John D. Rockefeller created the General Education Board in 1903, with the statement "I don't want a nation of thinkers. I want a nation of workers". Schools were to focus on causing children to Obey Authority, Follow Rules, and Memorize, Not Think, to work 9-5 for major corporations. The American President Woodrow followed this up when, in 1909, he addressed the New York City High School Teachers Association:

"We want one class of person to have a liberal education, and we want another class of persons, a very much larger class of necessity in every society, to forgo the privilege of a liberal education and fit themselves to perform specific, difficult manual tasks."[14]

In other words, while we have the impression that the purpose of school is to teach our children how to learn, the reality is that its greater purpose is to limit the ability of its students to think, so they will be more easily managed and more compliant citizens of their future society. How the school manages this is surprisingly easy, as we shall discover.

All this we will come to explore in great depth, as we consider the consequences to our civilisation when school produces a 19th-century model citizen in a world becoming progressively controlled by artificial intelligence, and must therefore require a new model citizen having higher responsibility in how they think and behave.

Chapter Four

To understand the whole as of parts

As we shall discuss, the general parent in the past and today is not educated to realise the role they really play in their child's academic development. Those who are, are generally so because they were raised through academically minded parents, or had experienced the necessary shift in thinking themselves, often through a university education, and awoke to this need.

Parents who had neither experience, lived through the ignorance of trusting the school. We can see this in our case with the mother we discussed previously. She (like almost all parents) believes school will teach her child all he needs to know. So, from her point of view, she created her child, gave him all the love and security she could until he was old enough for school, and then turned him over to this arm of society in the belief that it would be responsible for his complete and successful intellectual development.

As parents will know, from their own experiences, how the struggle of their child in school will likely reflect how they will struggle later in life, so they are naturally anxious about their grades. When their child achieves less than their parents hope for them, in their concern of what job and life role they may gain, they blame the teacher. In their defence, the teacher blames the child's background. As we have mentioned, in an earlier time they blamed the genes the child inherited for their performance, although in our more liberal times they seek an explanation for this through a socio-economic framework. Yet, despite the diplomacy of this explanation, in essence, it is taken to mean the same thing. The real underlying cause of a child's performance is "officially" taken to lie in their inheritance.

Of course, the general school has improved in many ways since it was founded over 150 years ago, and the classroom environment that children of the 19th century would have struggled through is nowhere to be found today. However, despite the obvious differences between the classroom then and now, the underlying means by which children are taught and so assessed still follow the same basic theme. This was the crux of the problem of children learning in the past, as it remains so today, despite ideas of multiple intelligences and learning styles, neither of which changes the abilities of students to learn. This is easily witnessed when we see one or two students leaving the classroom with full knowledge of that lesson, while the rest of the class will leave it with varying levels of uncertainty about what they were taught.

As we may now see, the belief in inheritance underlies our whole understanding of intelligence. So, when a child displays some sense of limitation in their learning, or when one child regularly performs better or worse than another, this is readily taken to be evidence of an inherited capability. All this seems a natural consideration to us. After all, when we try to explain some point to another and they consistently struggle to understand our mind as well as we do, we think them less able. Alternatively, when we engage with another who injects insight into our mind and describes our thoughts with great clarity, we feel they are cleverer than we are. Such is the mindset of intelligence. Any mention of intelligence inspires comparison, because this is what it does. Intelligence causes people to compare the actions of one to those of another. By such judgment, focus is brought far more upon the performance that is witnessed than how and why it has developed.

So, we envisage a teacher explaining a point of a lesson. They will ask individuals questions, and by the average response they obtain, they will judge how well the class as a whole has understood them. After this, or some time later, they will set questions and mark the effort that is returned to them. The different qualities of work they receive will be said to be caused by effort and natural ability.

The problem is that while some effort is noticeable in the stress and strain displayed, the inner workings of the individual's mind to relate what is new to what is known will not be, and in not being so will be largely passed over as a process determined by natural ability. It is the belief in this and the acceptance of it that is largely the cause of students being poorly developed in their learning, with the consequence of too many failing their education, and if not this, then failing to get the grades they would need to make their dream job become possible.

However, if we could move away from this snapshot impression we have of a child's or student's ability, we would be more inclined to consider the complex history of their emotional and linguistic development.

These are set about the strategies the individual has built up to be sensitive to recognise and associate with information as they determine relationships and through which they weave each and every part of their understanding into a structure that earns them their recognition from us.

As we may begin to gather here, any act of thinking is not simply a case of a student reading and then responding. It is an interwoven process of many complex factors with a product that is much misunderstood, for the case is not how good a student is by the result they give but how well they explain their mind. Those who are good with language skills will give a detailed argument to defend their thoughts, while others will say "I don't know" when they know something but lack the skill or confidence to better explain themselves. While these different responses will be used to evaluate the ability of each student and so reasoned to be traceable back to genetic differences, they are in fact purely developmental.

Thus, we will watch and judge how a child learns, and we will assume the stability they display in this to be a factor of different children having inherited genes of different qualities. Yet, the story of education has far too many instances where a child who performed poorly was taken out of their class, given different teachers, and moved into an environment with different children to produce, suddenly and dramatically, a totally different level of ability. In our account, we will discuss many such children. I was once one of them.

As I have mentioned, throughout my entire school career, I never reached more than the average level of performance and was more often far below it. I was the perpetual underachiever. When I was 19, I went back into education and became the top student in my college, achieving nearly 100% pass rates in all of my examinations. One lady whom I discussed this with told me of her failure in school. She explained how she hated mathematics as a child, and finished her education with very poor certificates. Was the cause of her performance related to some genetic variation? No! She had once been very good at mathematics, enjoyed it, and found it fun trying to solve various equations.

All this was until she was confronted with a bad-tempered teacher, who ridiculed her in front of the class because of a simple mistake. She never got over that humiliation. Ever since that moment, she avoided every question and had no confidence to discuss with other teachers things she did not understand. Because of that single incident, she became a grey figure in a background of variations that had nothing to do with effort or inheritance. Later in our account, we will explain why this is so, as we describe how the trauma of that moment so changed the chemistry in her brain that it affected the ability of her neurons to process information successfully.

So, we come back once more to think of the boy whom we began our introduction with, for we may better consider now that the dyslexia said of him and of the genetic quality behind his performance may otherwise be explained through numerous social factors. He may, for instance, have been raised with very poor language skills and so see the world too narrowly, or he may have been emotionally disturbed by some domestic stress. The mother gave insight to this possibility. We know the child is bullied, and this would certainly disturb his ability to concentrate in his lessons and so explain this inability he projects to others. There again, his low ability could be the result of a combination of many or all of these factors.

The point that we stress here is that any stability a child shows in low performance, however low it may be, providing they are otherwise normal in all features, cannot be so easily explained as having a genetic base, despite the common belief that it can. After all, the academic performance of any child in school is based on a very long and a very complicated history. Therefore, to talk about variation of ability in a class does not necessarily imply there has to be a genetic base for this. Such variation of performance, the different marks students are awarded, could be caused simply by the complicated relationships of confidence and insecurity since birth woven through their language development.

As we may begin to realise from this, performance in school, and so intelligence in life, is far more a factor of the environment than our impression of genetic inheritance, and so genetic diversity allows us to consider. In fact, as our account progresses into *"Intelligence: The Great Lie,"* we will come to discuss an alternative view of what the word "inheritance" could mean in intelligence. It will be very significant when we do this to know that Wilhelm Johannsen, the scientist who discovered the role of the environment in genetics, insisted that the word "inheritance" should never be used in any discussion of genetics.

Equally, in *"Brain Plasticity: How it Works,"* we shall come to understand how the circuitry of the brain works, and so how intelligence may be understood through a combination of the sensitive mind working with neurons and synapses to create networks of understanding. As we discuss this, so will we better understand the view of brain plasticity that was recognized by the founder of neurology, Ramon y Cajal. These will be essential reading if we are to understand how to begin to change the operation of the school and so the way teachers teach.

However, since it is widely believed in education that intelligence is something the child is born with that limits their ability, it will be a major part of our discussion in this book to explain how it is the actual mind of the student that fosters this ability. As we realise this, so will we come to discover that intelligence is not what many people think it is, and while we use this word freely to define the difference in the abilities of individuals, it is only a concept. We shall come to consider an alternative explanation.

One key to understanding what this may be, and how it may work, lies with language. Once we examine how a primitive Amazonian tribe does not have words for numbers beyond one, two, and many, we will understand why their intelligence is restricted so that they cannot understand what three, ten, or forty-two means. This does not mean that they are less intelligent than we are. It means that their perspective of what intelligence is is vastly different from ours. The intelligence of these people, just as that of all people, is greatly decided by the language they share. So, we find in our societies that the more words infants acquire, the higher their later performance in school is likely to be.

In essence, then, intelligence means different things to people of different cultures, and by the same rule so to people of different levels of society, as it is essentially defined by the language of their work. This has great implications for the difficulty we have in comparing the actions of different people, and so believing that such differences can be indexed and thereby said to be measurable.

Consider that intelligence is only our perspective of the end result of very many neurological and psychological components coming together in another human being, when they respond to a situation the way they have personally evolved to do so -- through their perspective of the world. Our greatest mistake in this is to assume that the mind of another sees the same world as ours does. It does not. The mind of each lives in the world it has developed through. Intelligence, as we may begin to grasp, is neither a singular feature nor a singular function of the brain.

Intelligence is the product of many components, many of which are similarly shared with our behavioral features, as each enables the human being to survive in a fluid environment. We can see this simply by how we visualize actions, evaluate from past experiences, and respond sympathetically to our benefit. Whether we are solving a problem with distance and time, conveying our understanding in writing, or seeking harmony with another human being, our mind and our brain will see these as part of the external world they learn how to develop through.

I try to explain this relationship by what we may call the intelligence-emotion-behavioral link. Through this, we may gain insight into why emotional sensitivity, developed through behavioral incidents, can influence the emotional sensitivity by which intellectual aspects of the environment are recognized, selected, and processed biologically to psychologically create what we call intelligence. We have already gained a small insight into this.

From the understanding that gene codes vary has come the statement that "all children are not born equal." There is a great deal of misunderstanding and ignorance behind this view, because it uses the example of genetic mutation (i.e., a child with Down's syndrome) to explain the normal genetic variation in a class, and so in a society with political overtones, as we saw in our previous chapter.

As we have just suggested, intelligence is not a singular feature, and so it is not inherited as such. The human being will inherit numerous components that will enable this "concept" to exist, but the genetic variations associated with these do not imply that they will naturally vary in quality within a population. Such variation may only be the shuffling of designs, which may not create differences in the quality of the feature the genes are responsible for. To the surprise of many, genetic diversity does not necessarily imply gene codes of different quality. It can merely mean codes of alternative designs.

Language is a very clear example of such inheritance, as we have mentioned. Even though language plays a vital role in the existence of the intelligence process, all human beings, regardless of genetic variation in this, will be genetically unrestricted in their development of this skill. The ability to learn to understand another human being is purely a developmental factor based on experience and is not dependent upon any type of genetic variation.

There are, as we shall see, many other genetic instructions whose natural variation in a population does not affect the development of their feature. The ability to perceive movement and so recognise change is another very important example of this. The biological construction behind this feature will be determined by the efficiency of environmental signals the brain receives in the early stages following birth, but competency with it will lie in the strategies the child's mind devises to recognise information, as they are emotionally interested or distracted at any one moment of perception. The ability to know of what something is and how it relates to something else is a further example here of inheritance not determining ability, just as is the ability freely to adopt a different view of a thought process. While we may think of intelligence as how quickly an accurate response is given, we may also know that this involves complex processing systems such as visual search and encoding, not to mention attention, and that these rely upon developed procedures and experiences.[15]

In further books, we will introduce the idea of common schemas that are indiscriminately inherited in each individual to enable them to develop the basic components that create an act of intelligence. Intelligence we must be aware, is not simply the performance we witness. It is a highly complex developmental process. As all the parts of the human jigsaw come together, so will we come to understand how and specifically why language and emotion drive the quality of intelligence in the normally functional human being. Poor qualities of these immediately after birth, as a lack of facial experience with the mother, can deprive the newborn of knowledge in how to develop normal communication skills. In turn, this can lead to attention deficiency disorders later in life, such as ADHD.[16]

As we will come to see, the words genetic diversity and inheritance can easily confuse our understanding of the intelligence process. We have just witnessed an example of this when we saw how certain components of intelligence develop their proficiency purely through development. Of course, there are genetic mutations and neural injuries and disturbances that will affect an individual's ability for intelligence, but in these books, we discuss the development of the general child in their general education, as they will develop to operate and serve their society. As we do this, and so understand how our personality is freely constructed through experience, but regard intelligence to be limited in this, so will we understand more of the politics that lie behind intelligence.

As we move from this book into *"Intelligence: The Great Lie,"* we will come to understand why intelligence is not genetically inherited in the manner we have come to believe it is, and from this realise a greater understanding to how human ability becomes determined.

This will be very important to do, least because this reasoning is what is behind the conviction of the mother and the child's teachers we have just discussed that her son has a genetic based learning problem, and much more because the philosophy it breeds gives design to the way all children should be taught in their lessons and how their effort is to be evaluated.

In short, this reasoning decides how the population of a society will be raised to think, and consequently how they may be governed. This gives insight into a deeper purpose of education that is less obvious today than it was in earlier times.

To begin to understand how children in a class can otherwise create different performances, and so ultimately play a better role in the democratic process, we may see that many of the problems with children who perform poorly in school lie in how they perceive information. By the quality of their language and the emotional aspect of how they decipher what information means to them, the individual sets in motion the mental and neurological processes that give this information meaning to those who are judging them. This is dependent upon the mental processes they have developed through and are subsequently able to better manage. School performance, as we will come to see, has nothing to do with intelligence, at least in regard to those who are not born with a physical impairment.

If we may see that the ability of this mother's child, who cannot read properly, can be explained purely through developmental factors, and Feuerstein's cognitive developmental system has demonstrated such a possibility with over a thousand worldwide case studies,[17] then the belief put forward to explain his inability as a factor of inheritance was wrong. To understand that this reasoning occurs regularly with poor performers, causes us to be wary of how we refer to the role of genetics in intelligence, and so the principle still today in how children are taught in school.

Significantly, then, we are forced to realize that the performance differences of any children in any class, in any school, could be created by factors other than the genetic bases they are usually linked to. Variation in academic performance, we shall see, is an extremely complicated issue that has far more causes than those of effort and inheritance, which are simply used to explain it.

Intelligence is a very complex process, whereby many different components interact. By envisaging how each component has developed and how each has learned to find relevance with another, so may we see how it is not so easy to explain differences in performance, and so intelligence, through a genetic base. With this realization, it will become increasingly apparent how and why intelligence only appears to be stable in the way an individual acts. Once we can realise what this means, then we can understand how a different approach to teaching could raise both the academic performance and intelligence of a class dramatically. We will see how this may be achieved in our final two books of this series.

Therefore, if education were to teach in a more effective way and teach its students how to understand their lessons, rather than demanding they remember things they don't understand, it would provide a paradigm shift in the quality of its product, and so in the citizens of the future.

This is drastically needed, for while these books will discuss how intelligence comes to be and how school works, the real purpose of doing so is to discuss how the children of today can be better prepared for their world of tomorrow. While we have explained that competence of learning in school is not directly related to intelligence, it would help us in our journey by understanding more about what is thought of intelligence.

Chapter Five

The Individual and Their Intelligence

In attempts to show that the genetic value of a human being's intelligence can be known, many tests have been conducted on infants and even babies, for at this time of life the influence of the environment is said to be very minimal and therefore reasoned not to confuse the impression of what the individual is born with. While this reasoning completely ignores the vital role of the mother's emotions affecting the personality and so the subsequent interactive skills of her fetus, let alone the equally vital language experiences of the neonatal, it needs to be realized that all such tests failed to find any recognizable stability in intelligence during the early years of life.[18] In fact, before the child enters the educational system, they do not display any stability or recognizable characteristic in their intelligence that is reliable enough to permanently compare one to another. Whatever predictions have been made upon the intelligence of a young child, later years have shown this prediction to be completely meaningless.

Why intelligence appears to be stable once the child has entered the educational system will become apparent once we come to understand the rules they are taught to make sense of information, and how they struggle to use these in the self-limiting and conditioning world of the classroom. However, before this, we need to understand how intelligence comes to be, where it starts, and how it develops.

Howard Gardner suggests that we have nine different kinds of intelligence,[19] but in our account, we see many of these as socially determined. While this may be said of intelligence in general, we will go far deeper in our discussion of intelligence than understanding it as a social modality, because this does not explain how it really works.

In a process, which we define as 'The Andersen Model of Intelligence,' we do not see human intelligence and the environment as two separate factors, nor do we see the brain learning to make sense of the environment. Instead, we take the view of the mind driving the neurons and dendrites of the brain to make their connections through the play of neurotransmitters, which it drives through emotional and self-seeking security issues.

In this way, each individual sees their own perspective of the world, which they learn to share with others through language. It is for this reason that we will see intelligence as a language process by which the individual first learns to recognise facets of the world about them and then present their meaning of these as they share their thoughts with others. It is by the vastness of experience and the degree of accuracy in this that the individual gains proficiency. It is very important at this stage of our discussion to understand the importance of sensitivity in how information is first recognised and then how thoughts are shared through a quality of sensitivity. More than any other factor, sensitivity in awareness, we shall come to see, is the key to understanding intelligence and how it and a student's performance in class can be improved.

Very simply, in school, we can say that the child will be evaluated on their response, and while it is understood that this response relies on how well the child understood information, little consideration is given to how they know how to explain themselves. Knowing information, and knowing how to explain this to another, is not the same thing. Yet, because language evokes social issues, as well as cultural ones, it is kept outside the evaluation process of intelligence, and so its true role in this is ignored. All this will become clearer once we become involved in the politics of intelligence. Setting this aside here, we may understand that these books will see intelligence through a biological and a psychological perspective, and discuss how emotional chemistry drives them both, as this in turn is driven by language. Language is not just words. It is also the feelings of security or insecurity created by one in affecting the emotions in another and so their personality as their mind ever seeks to develop.

In a biological sense, we see the brain and its sensory systems formed through the internal environment of the body (the food and drink consumed), and externally by the light and audio waves that stimulate the brain. While the living brain is always receiving this information, it is the mind that devises processing systems of efficiency. As the mind does this, it struggles to maintain its identity with information it has previously processed against how it defines new information. The mind's ability to define new information and so the uses it can make of this are compounded when the personality of another is incorporated into this process, so that we can see again how and why language determines the development of intelligence. Apart from such social language, intelligence is dependent upon two main components. These are strategy and emotion. Strategy decides how information will be processed, and emotion decides how accurately this will be done.

While these both begin to form during the foetal stage, there is no time in the life of the individual when they cannot be completely redesigned. Before birth, and indeed soon after it, these features are brought into a porto-formation to enable them to exist. However, the abilities they construct are forged through the real-life experiences of the human being, as their world unfolds before them. Both the strategies the human being constructs to understand and make sense of what is happening at any one moment, and their emotional state that gives sensitivity to these strategies, are continually adjustable. They are designed to be this way through the design of their genes, to ensure the human being can learn to survive.

However, the extent of this adjustability is not readily apparent because the brain requires stability in its operations. To obtain this stability, the brain relies upon the same strategies its mind devised in the past to deal with each new information it engages. It is because of this continuity in how the brain interacts with the outside world that the intelligence of an individual appears to be stable. In time, we will come to understand how the psychology of the situation conditions this stability, and how the plasticity of neural arrangements can change it. If the experiences of life are powerful enough, the intelligence of a person can dramatically change, just as their personality can. To understand how this can be possible, it is necessary to move away from the 19th-century idea that the intelligence of an individual is fixed by some inherited quality, and begin to realise when and how intelligence comes to be in the womb.

In 2009, scientists at Maastricht University in the Netherlands discovered that by the 30th week of gestation, fetuses are able to remember a sound for ten minutes. By the 34th week, they could remember a sound for four weeks.[20] We may understand from this that by the 30th week of gestation, the fetus has an active memory.[21] Since we cannot have intelligence without memory, we may take this time as the approximate start of our intelligence, for while we are still in the embryonic sac, we begin to learn.

We learn at this earliest stage of our life how to respond to diffused light, the sounds we hear, and the movements we make by which we learn to be mobile as we touch the walls of the womb, grasp the umbilical cord, and hold a toe. Despite the seemingly limited stimuli available to the fetus, they are surprisingly active as they learn to explore, record, and respond to their environment.[22]

Yet, before this time, the fetus will have developed to be sensitive to the emotions of their mother. From a very early stage, the fetus can pick up the emotional vibrations of their mother and know when she is happy or when she is stressed. In time, they will develop to hear the voice of their mother, and the external sounds around her. By each degree of these, the mother's unborn child will absorb this information into the scaffolding they are creating for their emotional chemistry.

There is a statement commonly made that "children are born differently." It has the meaning that each is limited according to their different genetic line, and so can never be caused to be equal in life. It is a sentiment anchored in the medical ignorance of the 19th century, when the workings of the brain were quite unknown. Today, we know that the fetus can undergo 300 genetic mutations prior to birth.[23] If we add to this how we know how the personality of the fetus is given foundation through the emotional experiences of its mother,[24] this statement takes on a whole new political angle, because now the inference is on after birth development instead of limitation to a genetic family line.

However, once the baby is born, they will have a means to remember information and be able to relate this to how they emotionally feel. This enables them to learn through the sensitivity they feel in the environment in which they move. It is vital that we realise that the threshold levels for their emotional chemistry will still be undecided. It will take the experiences of many, many years before these levels become settled to enable the child a level of stability in how they perceive and how they interact with the information of their world.

Emotion underlies every single act of intelligence.

From the moment they are born, and indeed before this time, the human being will relate to information through their emotional contentment of each situation. As the baby matures into the infant, and so into the child, they will provide sensitivity in their skills of interaction. When they are calm, collected, and fascinated, these skills will be very sensitive, as the child happily explores and makes discoveries. However, when the child is frustrated, depressed, or worried, the converse will occur, and what was once a happy and sensitive exploration of information will change into fleeting, half-broken grasps of disoriented images. This paragraph gives us our first real insight into the meaning of sensitivity in awareness.

After birth, the baby, and so the infant, will begin to develop their strategies to deal with information, as they visually, audibly, and through touch learn the differences between animate and inanimate objects. By the experiences of their interactions, the infant will devise skills to explore their new world, and bring into operation strategies that will seek to gain their acceptance from others for their protection. The quality and effectiveness of these strategies, and the skills they are developing, will lie in their sense of emotional security. Indeed, throughout the whole of their life, beginning from the earliest moment, each and every experience they encounter will be determined through their emotional contentment. It is for this reason that each and every act of intelligence a child makes will depend upon how their emotion relates to the situation at hand. Central to the development of their emotions will be the role of the caregiver, as they demonstrate and explain meanings with sensitivity through the language they use. John Fiske well put meanings to words when he wrote:

"What is the meaning of the fact that man is born into the world more helpless than any other creature, and more in need of a much longer season than any other living thing, the tender care and wise counsel of its elders?"[25]

Yet, just as the loving, emotional, and sensitive guidance of an adult is pivotal to map out the intelligence of the child, so is it equally recognized that children who are abandoned, abused, or neglected will fail to develop normal levels of intelligence.

One of the most dramatic examples of how emotional neglect can create extremely low intelligence was witnessed when Romanian orphanages were opened up to investigation in the 1990s. Inside these orphanages were found children who existed only in a zombie-like state. These children were totally unable to relate to the world about them, simply because they had been severely deprived of love and attention.[26] These children had not experienced emotion, and because of this, they did not have it. They were emotionless. They were lifeless. However, they did not respond to the efforts from those who discovered them simply because they had been deprived of emotion, although this was the most significant factor missing in their development, and also because they had never been taught the language of interaction. They did not know of the skills to interrogate and respond to information. These children did not know how to think because no one had guided them in how to do this.

The meaning here is to see how extreme cases give an example of the normal process by which intelligence is affected in its development by positive and negative perspectives of life. Understanding this will begin to explain a deeper role of the environment, and so a greater understanding of why intelligence is less determined by inheritance than we think. The environment of a child, of course, is defined for them by those who raise them.

As obvious as the role of the parent in developing the child's intelligence is, many young parents today seem to be unaware of how to do this. I recall, as I write this, once sitting in a doctor's surgery and watching one mother pick up a storybook, which she then shared with her 4-year-old daughter. The child was absorbed in the interaction, as her mother asked what she thought about this and about that. As I waited, another mother appeared with a child of a similar age. This mother spent all her time sending text messages while she waited for the surgery. Her child was active and wanted attention. The only response this child got was: "Be quiet!" "I've told you before ... keep still!"

In another incident, and one that will have some significance in our following book, I was traveling on a long bus journey. On the way to my destination, a mother boarded the bus with her infant in a pram. She gave love and attention to her child whenever it was needed. In time, another mother boarded the bus with her child of about the same age, and virtually ignored her child throughout the whole journey.

On the return journey, a mother and father entered the bus with their son, who again was of a similar age. I was amazed to watch this father, because he took the infant out of the pram and immediately began playing all kinds of stimulating games. He would lift his son to allow him to see over the seat in front. Then, he would move him down so he could not see, then he would lift him up again. Throughout the whole time they were on the bus, the father was constantly inventing different kinds of stimuli for his son. These were all fun and were all conveyed with meaningful love.

Most remarkably, the father then began to gently sing a song in Hebrew. I did not know the wording, but I could understand this was an act of transference. The father was chanting some kind of harmonic melody to his son while he was playing with him, and not, as we may imagine, trying to cause him to sleep. The calm, peaceful learning experience I witnessed here was one this father had obviously been raised on himself, or it had been strongly impressed upon him by others, presumably of his culture. By peaceful humming and teaching his son to be aware of information, the father was practicing the art of sensitivity in awareness very well. We will discuss this in great depth later.

While we take it for granted that parents, and especially mothers who have more time with their child, would naturally want to share their world with them, this is sadly not always the case. Today, many young parents are so absorbed in text messaging, Internet surfing, TV soap operas, and game shows that they too easily neglect to develop basic communication skills within their children.

In the UK, for instance, over a million young children in school, about two or three in each class, suffer from speech, language, and communication difficulties that were brought about through poor parental skills.[27] It is a little more disturbing to realise that because of these poor parental skills, an increasing number of 4-year-olds entering the school system today do not know their own name.[28] One of the problems in learning is orientation. This is for the child to know where they are in the progression of information. In a class of children who are constantly comparing and challenging each other, the identity by which a child sees themselves is very important when they are learning.

In the autumn of 2014, researchers at University College London published a report on the ability of pre-school children to commence their formal education in England. Having tested 5-year-old children in areas of reading, numeracy, and linguistic skills, as well as social and emotional maturity, they found that nearly half of them (48%) did not have the level of intellectual, emotional, and physical development to begin school. In fact, in some areas of the country, they found that almost 70% of children lacked the basic awareness necessary to begin school life. The report saw poor parental skills to be the main cause of the children's low developmental condition.[29]

What may be very obvious from this is the importance of the skills of language the young child is raised in, because their later academic performance can be related to these. Language, as we may have already understood, is not just a matter of vocabulary. Language here relates to all senses of communication, including the interactive (thinking or "hands-on") strategies the child witnesses and absorbs, and so the exposure to vocabulary it witnesses. As we mentioned, Hart and Risley conducted a great deal of research to be able to demonstrate how the performance of 10-year-old children in school could be strongly related to the amount of words they were taught in the first 3 years of life. This zero to three-year timeframe, they found, can be equally related to the language skills of the parents, as a projection of their socio-economic status.[30]

May we begin to ever more understand from the little we have so far discussed why intelligence is not simply "a thing" the child is born with, and thereafter develops by their genetic limitation.

When we think it is, we place a worth on a child's academic performance by how they presented their effort to us. Yet, we know nothing of the strategies they used in this process, nor do we know anything of those who guided them, or of those who sought to devalue their impression of life by intimidation or bullying. Too little do we really understand how school performance is affected by the distorted emotions of others, as we see the child and their ability detached from the world that gives it shape.

Thus, we see intelligence as a thing the child does or the way they act, and expect the same from them with any interaction they will make in the future. The fundamental mistake Spearman made when he invented the "g" and "s' factors of intelligence. We simply do not understand that intelligence is only a small act of one moment of time, and in our prediction of this skill, we fail to understand the self-limiting and conditioning world the child moves through.

Such an act of intelligence as we confuse this with the response a student makes is not evidence of the way they were born. Each act of intelligence they make relies upon the components they select to use, and the manner they have learned how to use these. Our later discussion on the rules of school will have great relevance to this. Therefore, any act that we assume is one of intelligence is only the summation of a large number of components. We know very little of this, even though these components enable this act of performance to exist and operate.

There are, as we shall eventually see, very many of these components, in which we have already introduced strategy and emotion, as they came into being and operate through language. Yet, even though the language of poor socio-economic children is well related to their low academic ability,[31] the great significance of this is unknown to those parents in general.

Chapter Six

The Importance of Words

As we have just demonstrated, different parents, often by their development, raise their children with their level of language. A very easy way to equalize the disparity in the language differences of parents, and so a means towards equalizing the academic ability of all children, is through storytelling. Storytelling is a very important way to develop the child's sense of language.

Finland, it may be noted, has a very successful educational service, and great emphasis is placed on early storytelling to prepare the child for their academic development.[32] The mother of every newborn child in Finland is given three books on mother-to-child storytelling from the state, to encourage their awareness of this.[33] Stories, it may be understood, are fundamental to a child's development, as they teach the child how to develop skills of sharing their thoughts and understanding how to relate to those of others. They establish oral skills, increase vocabulary, improve word recognition, and enable children to plan a composition of events, as well as to interpret those of another.[34] Stories, we may know:

- increase the number of words children know.
- raise a child's familiarity with words.
- cause children to recognise how words link, and so give words higher levels of association.
- improve a child's ability to more readily grasp a meaning given to them.

- teach children how to put a series of events in order, to present their meaning.
- improve their awareness that different people want to hear their mind in different ways.
- teach them how to better formulate their thoughts.
- improve their level of articulation and means of expression.
- inspire their imagination. Imagination inspires the confidence to want to explore. In turn, this creates the courage for the child to take risks, and thereby develop through mistakes learned.

In short, stories develop a child's ability with language. A child's ability with language underlies their means of competence in all the subjects of the school curriculum. Every composition and essay they complete, every history or geography assessment they hand in, and every mathematical equation they present in physics and chemistry is given worth by their ability to explain events as they tell "their" story. The importance of storytelling was borne out by a UNICEF study, which found that children who read better at 7 do better in intelligence tests later in life than children who do not read as well at this age.[35]

Later, we shall discuss a child I was introduced to by his teachers who regarded him to be mentally sub-normal. As I discovered that his parents had never told him one story in his life (this is really true), I explained to them the importance of this and how they should immediately begin to develop his imagination. Instead of the child being left to find his own bed, once the television had itself gone to sleep, the parents began to sit with their child and entertain his mind. Firstly, they read from books. Once they had experience of how a story is organized, I encouraged them to create stories from the child's suggestions and then allow the child to end the story by his own imagination. We were all shocked to see how this child suddenly and quite dramatically improved in his schoolwork, partly on account of his parents now sharing a story with him at bedtime.

Due to the pressures of modern society, many parents today have allowed television and computer entertainment to take away from them this traditional time of mind sharing, so that what was once a normal occurrence has now become a too-often-lost art.

The more we discuss intelligence, the more we will come to see that it is by the awareness of how we distinguish elements of information, define what they are, recognise relationships, associate these to what is about them, and relate what we have selected to the quality of previous experiences that we recognise a situation and so configure an act of intelligence by the response we make. Performance is school is only this. The way we convey our mind to another is the way they will judge us, and so say what our intelligence is. It is important that we understand that our ability to recognise how information can be differently presented to others lies in our experience of stories.

The more we begin to understand what we shall come to refer to as the environment, the more we will realise how the brain and the mind learn how to understand what this means, and so develop different ways of interacting with it.

If we could replace the singular word "intelligence" with"thinking skills," we would be brought to consider a very different view of the same ability. By the incorporation of the word "skills," we become aware of developmental issues that are reliant upon sensitivity. If we can accept this, we would come to see this feature of our interaction with the world in another light.

An act of intelligence, from this perspective, would not then simply come from information that has built up upon previous information, with each interaction determined by an inherited quality. It would be more understood through the sensitivity by which information had been identified in the past, and by the sensitivity with which it is related to the moment at hand to give quality to the conclusion made of it.

As we explore what this really means, we do not discuss the intelligence of a child as a permanent feature within them. Instead, we think that each response they give is a separate act that builds up from the way previous experiences were handled. In reality, this is all we may do, and sense comes to this when we understand how each act a child makes follows the pattern they have developed to identify and process information.

They may, for example, select the most obvious information presented to them, instead of deliberating which is the most useful for the task at hand. They may not check each line as they progress through their answer to a math question, and finish without consideration if the result they have produced "looks" correct. In essence, they may trust information far too readily. When they do this, they produce the same level of performance in each class and obtain the same recognition. Therefore, when information is vaguely selected, or vaguely interpreted by lack of interest, or worry, and worry or distraction are prominent issues in child development, it will be mismatched when stored, and so less easily found again when seeking to recognise or solve a problem with it. In short, there will be very low levels of sensitivity in awareness demonstrated by such a child.

Competence with the processing of information is simply dependent upon the child being able to control distracting factors and having an intention to want to be involved with it. Thus, if children were taught to be more sensitive in the skills they use and were taught new skills, their patterns of interaction would change. They would better identify with information, and this would improve their awareness of what it is, and what may be done with it, and so improve the sensitivity with which information is dealt with.

May we begin to understand from this that how accurately and how quickly one child responds to another is not so easily said to lie in the genes they inherited -- despite the argument used in this by those of one social level or culture against the children of a different background from that in which they raise their own children. The word intelligence has always had a political agenda, which is why we should not apply it to a student in their learning.

Although we discuss how the brain develops in *"Brain Plasticity"* I would like to mention a little of this here. There are some neural circuits that develop within the brain through a purely genetic plan, but there are many more that are given their primary design, pulled into construction, and maintained in this through signal information conveyed through the visual, audio, and tactile senses. All these are selected and fine-tuned by the mind. In other words, they are formed and given quality in their operation purely and totally through environmental experience.

Therefore, when people place emphasis on the inheritance of intelligence, they do not know how the brain is formed or how it works. For example, the cerebral cortex is shaped differently in each of us as it is brought into construction through the worldly experiences of each. This is the part of the brain that allows us to interact with the outside world and so to think. As we have mentioned, the mind gives direction to neurons in how they connect, and so in building up physical networks, it gives shape to the brain.

If we extend this understanding to how the school is designed to work, we may mention that by the way teachers teach, students are caused to learn, and students are caused to ask the question "what." Thus, when struggling to learn, as they are caused to do, a student will most commonly say, "What should I do, Miss?" In other words, children are taught to wait for guidance rather than taught how to find their own bearings in a situation and to learn how to move forward by reflection.

As we mentioned, school globally follows a 19th-century political plan to create managers and managed citizens, which it does by essentially educating children to be compliant with the authority of their teachers, as this prepares them with a mindset to be more compliant and less fractious to their later managers in society and industry. Fichte (an earlier rector of the University of Berlin) indeed saw how education should aim at destroying free will, so that, after pupils have left school, they shall be incapable, throughout the rest of their lives, of thinking or acting otherwise than as their schoolmasters would have wished.[36]

It follows from this that by using this word "what" in such a manner, and understanding how the physical brain is constructed through the actual words used more frequently, we may realise how and why the physical design of the cerebral cortex is inclined in its actions to be reliant upon the guidance of another, rather than to be questioning and even to be argumentative. This is to say that as the brain is shaped by the language used, the way neurons are pulled into place, so is its efficiency steered. Thus, when the parent or the teacher causes the child/student to use the word "what," the child's frontal cortex will develop to cause the student to think more of using this word in their interaction with information, with the dependency that comes with this upon another. "What can I do, Miss?" "What is happening?" "Please tell me, what should I do next?" The child and future citizen is raised to wait for information from another, rather than to deal with the problem themselves.

However, if the child/student is raised more to use words of "How" and "Why," which live in the Limbic System, then their brain in general will think more of using these words as the student makes their interaction with information, developing them to be more inquisitive, curious and questioning in their actions.

The words parents raise their children on, according to their social level and work responsibilities, suddenly give a whole new meaning to the phrase socioeconomic differences!

While it might be said that critical thinking is much in vogue at the moment in school, it needs to be realized that the manner of its education brings very little, if any, constructive development to the thinking of the student. To do this, the student needs to be raised on such words as "how" and "why," as we have just seen, and to have a strength of confidence nurtured within them to so use these words openly. The development of the student's confidence to stand up and to openly question is a most important ability that the teacher can raise in their students, because it is only with this confidence that the words come alive, enabling them to be more critical of information. To realise how the brain is formed through the quality of language the individual uses, causes us to reflect more upon how students learn to relate to the world about them.

We may only know what information is by how we first develop, and later choose to perceive it through our sensors. So, by the processes we have adopted from others and refined with our personality, we identify, select, associate, and process information according to our experiences. Secondly, and this will have great importance to us later, because each individual will be driven by their personal interests to see different values in the same information; no two individuals may ever see the same value in something. By their different emotional interests and needs, each will hold a different perspective and see a different use to what is thought to be the same information for all.

To better qualify this, it is necessary to understand that the brain of the child is shaped through the ways their mind develops to interrogate and interact with information, as we have just been caused to realise. With each minute engagement they make, they will be attracted to or distracted from information, and the meaning it may have to them, by their emotional interests or concerns. Therefore, the ability of any two children to understand the same information will lie in the similarity or dissimilarity of their backgrounds, as each was raised to perceive and make sense of information differently. In other words, no two children think the same way, nor do they see the same meaning in information. Our error, when we teach and when we evaluate, is to believe they do.

Such a belief is based on studies of identical twins, but as we are to see, such studies have failed to recognise that identical twins invariably develop through "almost" identical experiences, where each copied from and learned through the other. It is in the ignorance of this that there is a failure to understand that a child from one social identity will see a very different perspective on the same information than a child from a different social identity. This, of course, will and must be ever more so the case when two children are raised under different cultures, because their means of identification will be far more different. This is so because the understanding of the child, in how to identify and how to interact with information, is rooted in the language of those who raise them. In turn, their language is derived through the work, the social, and the cultural experiences that created their understanding of the world they live in.

We have mentioned this already, but the point needs to be stressed that when we mention language in the context of learning, this is not to mean the language of a people, be it English, French, Arabic, or Chinese. It is the codes that are shared through people that define what information is, and what uses it may have for them. This language explains how information interacts with other information, and it is defined by sensitivity. This sensitivity is much decided through the job skills people have, and the social and cultural perspectives that define their needs.

Therefore, while each individual child will see the world of information differently, as they interact with it from a personal and emotional perspective, the social and cultural group they belong to will have developed particular strategies to deal with their world that will be different from those of another group. By this understanding, the intelligence of individuals may be grouped through the similarity of their social and cultural experiences, as these will be defined through the language they have created. None of this will be significant to children until they enter education. However, once they do, it will be very decisive, because their "language of understanding" must, to some degree, be different from the language that was selected for the education that will serve them.

We may understand by this that when the language of their lessons and the content of their textbooks is set to serve one group identity, then children who have that identity will be more in phase with its understanding than children of a different identity, be this social and more so when cultural. This will become evident when we discuss the problems poor white children, and more so Hispanic and African-American children, have in the American educational system. Nearly all countries, as it may be known, contain children from minority groups who struggle in their education, because their education system serves a different identity than theirs, which can be purposely done.

To this moment in our introduction, we have gained an understanding that the developing intelligence of the child is steered through the sense of security they have within themselves, and how they use this to regulate the strategies they have developed through those who influenced them. It is by how they can balance these two factors that they make sense of information, and so the world they live in.

All this will become apparent when we realise that a significant factor in students who do well in school is the love and guidance they receive from their parents. In addition to this, we have also gained an understanding that language is very important, because it enables items and the interactions they make to be defined with a purpose. May we see from this that as each child develops, step by step, through infancy and gradually into the childhood world of education, each will be differently prepared for what is said to be the same opportunity.

When we talk about intelligence, we do so in general terms. However, each child's value of this really comes down to the perspective they have of life, because the way the child develops to interact with information will generally determine how they will do this in adulthood. Unless some whirlwind changes their life, and this can happen, the early marks and later grades the child gains in school will determine the kind of work and the level of stimulation they will gain through this. So, a child who does poorly in school will obtain a job with low stimulation and live in a social world whose entertainment is suited to this. The opposite will be the case for a child who does well in school.

Therefore, any discussion of intelligence in education is really to mean the capability the student displays in the responses they give. Their ability in this really centers around the many forms of distraction they will struggle against in the classroom, and how well they adapt to overcome these. The greatest mistake a teacher can make is to think that all children in their class are constantly following their minds. They will not be. As one child will try, another will be wondering what they can do after the lesson. Just as one will be thinking of a bully who frightens them, so another will be thinking of the fight they witnessed last night between their mother and father, and wonder what their security in life will be.

Teaching children is really about bringing emotional harmony to a mass of individuals with different desires, who usually want to be somewhere else. Since the way children can be brought to focus their thinking in a class is a major point of our overall discussion, it will serve us well to dwell a little further upon this.

Chapter Seven

The Individual and School

Before school, the child embarks upon thinking adventures. They will play, and they will learn by themselves. However, how they see their world and how they believe they should interact with it will largely have been fashioned for them through the drives, stresses, and understandings of their parents. As they engage the world, and so write each page of their life story, the manner in which each child does this will be influenced by the sense of security and love they are raised under. As they see things, hear sounds, and touch items, the child develops a meaning to the world about them. They are attracted to some things and explore them, while other things pass them by. Before school, the child lives in a free world, where their mind is free to wander. What they like, they take interest in; what they do not becomes unknown.

What brings a unity to the free and distant minds of children is the system of school, because the school world employs definable rules by which a common understanding can be gained of information. These rules enable the child from the 3 dimensional world of home and play, to understand the 2 dimensional paper world of information. This is where intelligence or school ability formally begins, and also where it gains stability.

When the child enters this new world, they are indiscriminately and en masse taught rules by which they can relate to, and understand the information they must learn. As their lessons progress, the ability of each child to relate to the steady build up of these rules will much lie in their emotional desire to do so, and how they recognise how to associate each new rule to all those that went before it. Since every classroom will be a Babylon of minds, we may understand how each child struggles to make their sense of what is happening in a lesson.

As the only way the child can translate the meaning of another is through language, and so make their sense of these rules, we can see how crucial language is for their academic development. Their ability for this will be much decided by the similarity of the language used by school to the one they know. It is of no small matter to discover that the child's familiarity with the language used by their teachers, and expressed in their textbooks, will much decide how easily they can relate to the rules through which school operates.

These rules define the whole existence of the educational experience. They define how to orientate a book, or a sheet of paper on the desk. They tell the child the narrow end must be parallel with the edge of the desk facing them. They also tell the child how to hold a pen. Rules tell the child they must write only with blue or black ink, because red is reserved for those with authority. Rules tell the child where to set a letter on a page, how the size of one letter should be compared to the one it follows, and the one it will be preceded by. Rules define the phonetics of the letters of the alphabet, just as they explain what vowels are, and how they must be used. They define the syntax, grammar, and layout of a composition. Rules define numbers, and their relationships in mathematics. They explain what a mathematical equation is, and precisely how it may be operated.

Rules define the curriculum, and all the components of its subjects. Rules tell where the classroom is, and where the child must sit, and how long they must stay seated before they are allowed to move. Rules tell them the sound of the bell means they can be free, and rules tell them the second time they hear the bell means their freedom has ended. These rules are devised to bring order into the mind of the child. They are unbending and inflexible to the drives, needs, and personalities of the child.

With minds bubbling with energy, and with the personality of each desiring to be recognized for whom they do not know who they are, all children in a class look at their teacher and appear to be following the lesson. This is an illusion! It is more the case that as the teacher desires all minds to concentrate upon theirs, all those other and different minds will be pulled into quagmires of self-doubt, as they continually test each other, and search for conflicting interests in order to escape with happier thoughts. Over the years that pass, each of these minds learn their own balance between what the school wants, and what they want.

The child of nature will struggle against this conformity at first, some never stop, but as each is forced to comply, each takes note and value of these rules differently. Girls who are calmer settle into them easier, and so often do better later in school because of this. Boys, more with a mind to kick a ball or climb a tree, tend to take less note of them, and so generally do not do so well with them as girls, save for those who are myopic, because, due to their perspective of the world they are calmer in dealing with the relationships of information.

Children, may it now be realized, do not naturally think as school desires of them. They have to learn to acquire proficiency in this, which they can only do by the competency they know with the rules of school and how they use them. Consequently, some children come to recognise the codes that lead to this proficiency, and so relate to the world of these rules immediately. Others never do.

May we see that how well each child desires to make use of these rules, is given quality in guidance to do so, can resist distractions, and are free from those who wish to torment them, decides how well they concentrate and progress in their lessons. The importance of a student's competence with such rules is well explained further. However, as the free and causal mind of the child is forced to comply with the rules of this artificial world, the responses they give are used to usher them into a level of stability.

All this may seem very natural, and indeed it is, until we realise that while the child will be taught information in their school life, at no time will they be taught how to think upon it.

A teacher may hold up a sheet of paper to their students, and tell them that by cutting off one of the four corners there will be three left. Seldom, will they teach them to expect five corners to be remaining. Without being taught how to think about the information they are provided with, each child will be tied in their effectiveness to the skills of reasoning they were raised on.

Before and outside of school, the child develops through the personal interaction of those who foster their development. They take note of what interests them and ignore what does not. A question they raise, gains a level of response. So, through the guidance of others, they learn their own meaning of the world, and how they should interact with it.

The world of school is different. Now, the child has no freedom. They must learn what they have no interest in learning, and they must compete through the insecurities and challenges of other children, to grasp an understanding of information that never stops moving.

So, they will be introduced to different shapes, and be told that one is called a square and another a rectangle, and be much left to their own desires and interests to recognise the differences between these. As each child is much left to make their own sense of information in school, so the ability they develop lies in how it has developed. As we will come to see, performance in school, and the intelligence that is mistakenly associated to it, is caused to be stable by the self-limiting and conditioning world of education.

This conditioning world is purposely designed to stabilise and route children. School is rules, and how well the child is prepared for these before they enter this system, and how they can then concentrate and work with each, as each is disclosed to them, much decides their performance. According to the grade with which school rewards them for their compliance, each child will leave this institution to take up a working role and serve their society, either as a manager or as a managed.

- This is school. This is how it works, and this is its purpose!

As we have mentioned, it is the emotional perspective of the mind that guides the strategies it makes, which enables information to be deciphered and processed. From neonatal to death, it is the state of the mind's emotion that causes the individual to be sensitive in how they explore their world, and how they give attention to detail. At no other time in their life is this situation more decisive than during their years in school.

When the child is calm and happily attracted to information, they explore it in detail. The more interested they are, the more they notice finer details. The more they engage other information, the more they notice how parcels of information differ. The more fascinated they are, the higher is their skill in identifying relevant details within the array of information present. By the sensitivity in how they compare these details to information they have stored in their memory, is the means by which they conclude an action to take.

As we have said, knowing of information is only part of the story. The other part relates to how well the child can explain their mind. It is, after all, by how well they explain their mind that judgement will be made of them. Knowing how to do this, demands that they know and are familiar with the rules that have been decided for this. As their competence with these acts is rewarded, so their personality gains esteem, and they come to realise with each act of intelligence that they know who they are. Yet, as much as their fascination drives them to engage information with delicate sensitivity, their worry upon another issue can so distract them from this that they can suddenly register nothing about it.

Thus, words that moments before flowed smoothly on a paper the student was reading and made instant sense, suddenly became disconnected when a shadow of fear fell upon their mind. When worry seeps into their mind, they may read the same sentence again and again, and each time become more convinced it is written in a mysterious language, as they fail to grasp the meaning it is trying to convey. Equally, the spoken words they hear that make sense, because they are clear and precise, become unrelated as they are driven into a distant fog by fear. Fear does this. It floods the child's brain with chemicals that confuse their attempt to think in detail.

Further on in this book we explain how on a survival level, these chemicals instruct them to flee or fight. On the level at which the child learns in school, these hinder their effectiveness in processing information. Thus, fear, worry, and concern are degrees of a process that cause the child to think more upon their survival, be this physically or socially, than factors of lesser importance. Fear relates to a danger to their existence, while worry relates to the concerns they have of others hurting or rejecting the image they have of themselves.

How their behavioural skills relate to the ways of others are decided by experience, and it is by experience that they regulate the chemicals in their brain to control their emotions. A child who daily carries some worry, because they are picked-on in school or secretly carry a domestic trouble, will concentrate less in their lessons than those who have more transient worries. In time, we will come to examine how such long-term concerns can cause permanent changes to the chemistry of a child's brain.[37]

- The effectiveness of a child to relate to information, and to relate this to their previous experiences, will be decided by the delicate balance between their interest with it, and their struggle to push some disturbing factor out of their mind. In Part Two, we offer strategies for teachers to handle this better.

Obviously, the deep fear of one can be the causal concern of another, just as easily as the other way around. Yet, the effect of this concern in the performance of the child is unknown to the teacher, as they struggle to compare and make assessment of each of the different minds in their class. All the teacher may do to make assessment of their students is to judge their ability through the stability they witness.

Because competence in school is seen to be based on intelligence, which is said to be partially inherited, any stability that is noted when a student processes information is said to be evidence of their genetic worth. With this being said, when the student responds to a question, the ability that is noted of them is said to represent all they ever were and therefore, all they may ever be.

The greatest error in judging an act of reason, especially when it is said to be one of intelligence, is to assume that what is seen must be seen. When we do this, we fail to understand the history of how the individual developed to this moment in time. By the same means, as we judge others by the quality of their actions and are impatient to recognise the significances of those who fuelled their drive, gave strength to their insecurities, and set direction for them in how the world in which they grew could be interpreted, so are we judged by our last act. It is this tendency to accept competence as an act of intelligence that encourages the belief that it is a stable and, therefore, an inherent feature of the individual.

When we talk of intelligence, we think of the brain, and we forget the role of the mind. As we have mentioned, it is important to realise that we do this because when we think of the brain, we think of a genetic model both developing and operating, which suggests and gives explanation for intelligence to be stable.
However, the reality is that it is the mind that brings the brain into efficiency through its desire to be aware of the environment. The ability of the mind to process information efficiently is dependent upon a factor of stability, because stability allows the ready association of what is new to what has been stored in the past. This stability is re-enforced by a secure and happy mind, but it is thrown into erratic instability when that mind is insecure and worried.

Quite simply, the mind loves stability. Since birth it has developed its own means of understanding the world, based on the responses it gets to the interactions it makes. As each interaction the child makes is decided by an element of emotion, each strategy they design and so employ in an act of intelligence is witnessed by them as a projection of their identity. It is in this sense of ownership, the actions by which the individual knows who they are that we see why and how psychology controls this stability.

Therefore, when a teacher observes how the same child in the same class makes the same mistake over and over again, they need to understand what is really happening within their mind, rather than dispensing a mark. The child's means of interaction, which the teacher witnesses when they examine their style of writing, notes their spelling mistakes, and how they struggle to understand how they related one point to another, will, after all, have developed over many years.

It is not simply that the individual learned to do one thing in one way differently from another individual, but that within the organisation of their brain a whole machinery will have been constructed. Specific neurons will have been targeted together to create the electro-chemical circuitry that allows strategies to develop. It is these strategies that enable the child to write, read, draw, and think the way they do.

Therefore, what is taken to be the stable and qualifiable intelligence of a child is really only their brain demonstrating stability in its operations. Without this stability, the brain would not be able to relate to events with any degree of reliability. We discuss this factor of stability in great depth in a further book, when we discuss the idea of critical periods. However, we may consider here that if the personality of the student can be inspired to change the way they make interaction, then their brain can learn how to rewire itself to allow this to occur.

Such is the act of learning, and it is based on knowing what to change and desiring this change to occur. If the desire is strong enough and if the guidance is earnest and sensitive enough, the level of performance, which is thought to be stable and unalterable, can be found to be highly alterable and of unlimited potential.

- It is very important to realise that even though others will see a strategy of interaction a student makes as wrong, if the mind of that student does not realise it to be so, despite the advice they are given, they will believe their way to be correct and hold to it. In believing this to be so, they will use this means of interaction for all subsequent experiences they engage.
- As one experience builds upon another, the strategies that were once gained through a personal perspective of how to engage information and how to respond to it become said to be evidence of their inherited quality.
- The willingness of a student to follow their teacher's guidance and change the strategy they use to interact with information will be much decided by how well they recognise the purpose of what they are asked to do, and how well they recognise what to change within themselves to accomplish this. All these stages are controlled and regulated by emotion as it is steered through language experiences.

When the student has the personal attention of their teacher for the time they need it, this process is more possible. Compound the attention the student needs by placing them with 30 or 40 minds, with each seeking their own guidance to understand better how they should change their strategies, and the extent of their success is obvious.

We have much to discuss about the methods of teaching that allow students to learn what is expected of them. Yet, we may see from what we have so far discussed that the relationship between the teacher and the student relies upon the language of the mind they share, and of their willingness to be adaptable to each other.

While it may be said that the teacher can be considerate to the difficulties of each student in their class, it is to be realised that under the pressures that condition them, they can too easily relate the student's language to theirs, and so judge their intelligence through this.

In this way, they regard the student who understands the language of their mind better than others to be the cleverest. By the same reasoning, they can just as easily regard a student to have a low level of intelligence, when they struggle to understand the language that student uses to explain their mind. Others are then seen as having average ability, when they are understood by them sometimes and not at other times. We experience this attitude in all encounters we have with other people, from how well they understand the street directions we give them to how they respond to any gesture we make.

Learning is a process of communication, and communication is the act of language. A quality in language, we have already explained, is not decided by genetic codes. Language is a developmental and purely learnable process. From the view point of language, learning can be seen through a process of two parts:

- In one part, it is how well the teacher attempts to understand the confused mind of the student.
- In the other part, it is how well the student can control the factors that are distracting them, to relate to and to understand each step of the information their teacher is giving them.

Neither one of these processes is easy. However, with the pressure of time, the teacher is too easily caused to regard the feedback they get as the student's natural ability to understand them. After all, they cannot guess the disturbing flow of thoughts that interrupt the concentration of their student. These thoughts, which are so vital to the student's understanding, can be fully receptive one moment and lost to some other thought, feeling, worry, or concern the next.

We may see from this that intelligence is seen to be limited by a genetic value partly because of the self-limiting world of education, but much more because the mind seeks a reliable means of operation from the brain. The mind then, trusts its history of strategies, over those of the mind of another; unless, as we have just mentioned, the individual feels emotionally able to trust another more than they do themselves. When they do, they absorb the strategies of others into their own, and so are better able to recognise rules they previously missed or misunderstood.

This is one reason why teachers who behave as instructors, and fail to secure this emotional trust, are less able to help their students to grasp the fine points they are trying to teach them, which would otherwise evolve the level of their ability. Most problems I encountered with students who did not understand something was found to lie in their resistance to the personality of the teacher who gave them the information, or with an emotional imbalance in that learning situation, than to the complexity of the information itself.

It arises from this that when a child cannot understand much of their lesson for whatever reason and finds no means to do so, they tend to protect their identity by role-playing to what is expected of them. We discuss this in more depth in further books, because this act of role-playing does create a real factor of stability in the student's academic performance.

As we will come to understand, one purpose of these books is to promote the need for the teacher to use the method of mediation in their teaching, which is a continual interaction of minds, although I have fine tuned this concept to seeing it through the Art of Sensitivity in Awareness. As we shall see, other methods of tuition, such as encouraging the student to learn by themselves through textbooks, tend to isolate the student from the mind of the teacher. Mediation, on the other hand, enables a failing in the student to be immediately addressed by the teacher, as both progress in a step-by-step manner through the learning task. In a later stage of our account, we discuss how a single teacher can mediate to 30 or 40 students in a lesson simultaneously, to teach each more successfully.

We have much to discuss in the importance of this, and also much to explain as to the understanding of what mediation really means. Mediation is more than just teaching small points that seem irrelevant to the student, and certainly not a means to restrict their freedom of inquiry as is mistakenly thought. Mediation holds the key to understanding a clear chain of thought sequences, which are necessary to fully comprehend the task at hand. This is more important today than it has been in the past, when parents can be too busy or too tired to teach their child how to associate with information. Mediation from the teacher offers the student a personal association with information. It is through the quality of this interaction that the immature mind can be guided to find themselves in the learning situation.

It is in lacking this personal identification with information that fuel is given to acts of apathy, rejection, and more increasingly violence in the classroom. As we may have grasped that emotion is the base of intelligence, then, so may it be obvious that if there is a good emotional understanding between the student and the teacher, then the student will more seek to learn from the teacher. This personal relationship is of paramount importance in helping the student not just to do better in education, but to actually stay in it long enough to obtain a worthwhile certificate.

As President Obama pointed out in his State of the Union address in 2011, a quarter of American children are not finishing their high school education, when half of the new jobs created within the following ten years will require a higher educational experience.[38] This, of course, is a global problem. Our problem then, is how to help the child to understand the importance of their education, because if they can do this, they will stay in it longer and try harder.

Mediation offers one solution to this, because it enables each to overcome their language troubles, and so would help them to gain greater relevance in their learning process. Since we understand that each child thinks differently to another, a subject that teaches children how to think would also help to equalize the opportunities for children to learn.

Educationalists such as Vygotsky and Dewey laid the base for children to be taught how to think a century ago, and those such as Lipman, Feuerstein, and more recently Baron[39] have pleaded the case for this, as I have made my own humble contribution. Without such instruction, each child must rely upon the reasoning skills they acquired from their parents and any help they can get from their friends to understand their lessons.

Both of these, a teacher who uses mediation and a subject that teaches children how to think, when both are based on the art of sensitivity in awareness, would improve the overall ability of children. It is my experience and my belief that this would achieve a dramatic rise in learning performance. In turn, this would lead to a higher generalized intelligence. This combination, as we shall come to see, will provide the solution that education is desperately seeking. However, we have much to discuss before we can understand the problems of education, to realise this, and then how it could redesign itself to the changes these will bring.

One of many hurdles to this lies in the reasoning that children learn best by themselves, which is a mistaken follow-up from Piaget's theories. This reasoning trusts that through their hands-on experience, children are better able to relate to the problem they are engaged in. While there is some substance to this, it needs to be better qualified, for to believe that children learn best only by themselves is not correct. To think otherwise is to ignore the history of child development and its dependency upon guidance. For as the baby, infant, and child rely upon guidance to learn how to understand their world, so does the older student. This is not to say that the individual needs the same level of guidance as they did when they were younger, it is to realise that as they develop such guidance takes different forms. Yet, whatever form it takes, it will always seek to reconstruct earlier parts of an individual's development that proves to be wrong or incomplete.

As each child will have learned to recognise information through different backgrounds, and think back here to how different parents behaved in the doctor's surgery and on the bus, we can understand how each child engages information with different processes of reasoning and different levels of sensitivity. Therefore, to let the child in school learn by themselves is to limit their understanding to the domestic and social world that formed their skills of intelligence. This will cause them to live with the information in their lessons, just as they do in their personalised home environment, but be evaluated by a system that ignores this. Let us turn our attention to the history behind education to understand why it operates the way it does today.

Chapter Eight

A System for the Masses

In our developed societies, we tend to take it for granted that all children have the right to gain an education, and that with this being so it is provided for their natural development. This opinion leads us to the reasoning that education, such as it is, is intended to be given "more or less" with equal provision.

Yet, if we examine the very rudimentary education that is offered to a large percentage of children in underdeveloped countries, especially where their economy is heavily dependent upon manual labour, as in agriculture or mining, we realise by their inequality that education is not intended to be offered as a natural right. Rather, education is provided as a necessity for the working operation of that society. Therefore, and in accordance with the level of technology and the social organisation of its society, education is directed to govern the development of its students, firstly to maintain that social operation, and then to match their abilities to the job task responsibilities predicted for them.

The organizational force behind each educational system does not require of it that it provide an output overwhelmingly capable of being professionals or labourers. In fact, since with the correct developmental background, one worker could reasonably perform the task of the other, societies implemented various strategies in society and education to create a general acceptance of the unfairness of opportunity for work. By doing this, the society maintained an acceptable variation of functioning ability in its workforce, while at the same time maintaining communal support for its operational harmony. It arises from this that the philosophies that were chosen to guide an educational system were not selected because they offered the best means of how each child could learn, but because they offered the cheapest means to provide all students with a basic education.

Any educational service may be found to have its roots in the actions of well-motivated individuals who sought to give children a better and happier life. This was to be achieved through a patient teacher working with small groups of children and having the time to give individual counselling where necessary. The idea here was for children to develop through open questioning, by which they could bring the mind of another into the ways their mind had developed.

However, once employers wanted to know how good their employees could be, and once the cost of running a vast public service was taken on board, there was too little money for this philosophy. Children were to be herded together in large groups and matched one against the other as quickly and as cheaply as possible.

Thoughts of why different children struggled to learn in different ways, and sought four classrooms with four teachers for each to teach 20 students, went out of the window. The idea that each child was born with their own brain not only allowed education to process children the cheapest way (now one teacher could teach 50 or more children in one room), but it also played to the political design of keeping children tethered to the social purpose of their parents. As we shall now move to understand, it was precisely this way of processing children that created evidence for the ready acceptance that intelligence was largely inherited.

By the adoption of a processing system, education was able to transfer the real responsibility for the child's development away from itself, and to the care, energies, and experience of the parents. In this way, the parents who were better prepared to raise their children were normally those who had been so raised themselves, and were aware of the skills to progress through education into university.

Thus, while some children were recognized as the brightest, it was only because they had been better prepared and coached to keep up with each lesson as it occurred. They were, for example, found to give total commitment, have good working habits, show confidence to take creative risks, and come from a secure and creative home. They also, of course, would have been taught to read and write before they entered school. To ensure that education was not to be held responsible for developing the many more children whose parents did not know how to better develop them, these developmental skills were said to be of less significance than those they were born with.

While the general public and, therefore, the normal parent were ignorant of such strategies, they were very well known by some educationalists. One man in particular strove to counter the impression then created that a child was only as good as the seeds they came from. Thus, J.B. Watson (a founding figure in American psychology) once wrote:

"Give me a dozen healthy infants, well-formed, and my own specialized world to bring them up in, and I'll guarantee to take any one at random and train him to become any type of specialist I might select, doctor, lawyer... and yet, even beggar man and thief, regardless of his talents, penchants, tendencies, abilities, vocations and race of his ancestors."[40]

Learning philosophies that centre upon awareness, as Watson was discussing, focus upon environmental development and recognise a greater plasticity in performance. The system they create requires greater guidance from the teacher for the students. On the other hand, systems that seek students to experience a "generalized" instruction and thereafter make their own use of this information by repetitive exercises, make less use of the teacher.

The former system enables each and every student a far greater means of finding their relevance in what they are learning. These students obtain a higher level of assistance to correct what was previously misunderstood, and so develop with greater purpose. Their intelligence can improve! The latter system relies less on the teacher for its effectiveness, and much more upon the skills passed to its students from their parents, their ability to control distractions, and the effort they make or are caused to make. Under these circumstances, the student's intelligence remains relatively stable and is relatable to the life experiences of the family that raised them.

Accordingly, when the task of education is to classify and train a mass of children with intangible and indefinable experiences, under a restrictive budget for different job purposes, the system using a "generalized instruction" fits the need. Such a system promotes the idea of a static ability, steadily progressing at its own rate. Under this purpose, the idea of a malleable ability developing through open-ended and guided experiences would endear education with more responsibility than it has the resources or the directive for.

This idea of a "fixed" ability has always been of greater preference to the system of generalized education, not only does it justify the operation of a deeply structured classifying system, but more notably it gives much license for a higher student-to-teacher ratio. After all, when emphasis for student performance is deflected away from the capability of the teacher, it seems inconsequential to increase the number of students in the class. Parents hearing that education is saving money by increasing this ratio believe that it is more efficient, which they translate to mean their child is getting a better education. The opposite is true!

While the student-to-teacher ratio has little meaning when the ability of those students is regarded as naturally limited, it has a very decisive meaning when their development is reliant upon a close liaison with the teacher, which it is. Beyond this, belief in a fixed or inborn ability deflects responsibility for poor academic performance away from the system that manages the teacher in their operation, and gives insight into deeper operational processes than are at first apparent.

A historical examination of an educational system would show in its setup and running, the existence of a struggle between educational forces that sought to devise systems of teaching reliant either upon students learning through awareness or through exercise techniques. The difference is both fundamental and crucial.

So, we find that while Danish education sees its founders as Grundtvig and Kierkegaard, the practical operation of the state education does not adhere to their philosophies, since these do not satisfy the harsh reality needed to classify children. So Denmark, like so many other countries, adopted the philosophy of the American Thorndike that enabled this classification, and subsequently that of the Swiss Piaget that brought it into another perspective, as both avoided the teaching of Grundtvig's "the living word."[41]

Accordingly, Danish children today sit in neat rows in class sizes, much the same as in any Western country today. Information is presented to them, and they are assessed on their ability to reproduce what they have learned, the way they have personally understood it. To think then, of the very many Danish state schools, is not to confuse them with the very, very few Folk High Schools that do operate on Grundtvig's principles, for the purpose of each is different.

To be fair to Denmark, its society makes a great effort to equalize, as much as possible, the social experience of learning. While it is true that Danish children are still a product of their domestic life, and driven by their own personality and sense of security to interact with information, they are much more on an equal plane than children of many countries. The idea of an equalized environment, at least in theory, does lend itself to differences in grades as a product of natural ability. However, in practice and in reality, the environment of each child is not identical, and while it is more equal in Denmark than in most countries, there are many diverse opportunities for different stimulation and experiences to explain how the environment is responsible for the child's grade.

Yet, the Danes, like the other Nordic countries, do try to equalize their social environment to create a more harmonious society. Others, as we shall see, purposely do not. Certainly, the Danish education is a happy experience for the child, due to its emphasis on social empathy. However, the outline process is the same as any country: the child is taught information, their competence is assessed irrespective of the quality of the teacher, and they are routed to one of many varied forms of higher education or released into the job market. All of this process is based on the belief that their performance is much a product of their natural ability.

Therefore, and as we have already mentioned, our discussion needs to consider the educational systems of different countries in a unified sense. One country may have a different political character from another, and although its politics will determine how its education operates, the underlying design of that education will revolve around the concept of inherited ability. In time, we will come to understand why this is so, but for now consider the shaping of American education.

A century ago, we would have found educationalists in America complaining about the inadequacy of its education. A leading figure at this time was John Dewey. Dewey wrote profusely about the necessity to teach philosophy and skills of reason[42] in small classes of eleven or so children.[43] Yet, it was not this reasoning that was taken to guide mainstream education. It was that of such psychologists as Thorndike, who saw the learning process as determined by trial-and-error strategies. Thorndike based his laws of how children learn and how they should be taught (The Laws of Effect, Readiness and Exercise) not on studying children, but on his observations of rodent behaviour in his experimental laboratory.[44]

So, Thorndike's principles of learning, which reasoned that children learn best by repetition[45] and so could be taught en masse, gained political sponsorship beyond Dewey's learning through guided experience, because they gave a neat formulation for the training and categorization of ability, which held better rein to finances.

It was because of this that American education, just as the educational system of any other country at that time, caused more than 50 children in a class to sit neat and terrified behind solid wooden tables, praying not to be noticed by the disciplinarian who, with cane in hand, always seemed to ask that which had not been memorized. As we may understand, this system was far more appealing than one that saw much smaller classes of children sitting around a mediator, developing their understanding through a questioning dialogue. Teaching through sensitivity in awareness, we shall see, is a process that radically disturbs the concept of potentiality being either stable or predictable.

It will now be of no small significance to learn that following an experiment on human beings instead of rodents, Thorndike subsequently came to reject his law of exercise. It was only after Thorndike had left his rats behind and moved to examine how human subjects he had blindfolded could not distinguish between lines of different lengths they had drawn that he was forced to admit the necessity of guidance in learning!

Dewey   Thorndike

By this time, however, it was all too late. The machinery of many educational systems had come to be reliant upon his principles, and had taken these as the foundation of their tradition; after which they could only be relatively flexible to new ideas and new thoughts.

There is a need to mention here that the study of animal behaviour, which we will see was often used to devise principles for how children should be taught and examined in education, is not appropriate to human behaviour. The ability of a rat, for instance, can be determined by the degrees of food or pain it is given, but human beings have a higher consciousness that causes them to be totally unpredictable to such evaluation.

A rodent can be frustrated, and this can affect its response. However, this frustration of a rodent, if it can be recognized to bias a decision, does not demonstrate the complexity of human response, either in performance or more importantly in the buildup of experiences by which stimuli is evaluated. To ignore this is to say a human being has the same consciousness, tolerance, benevolence, sensitivity, and is driven by the same subconscious desires and repressions as a rat. The point here is that each child is unique, and they are so because of how their environment has cultivated them. This will have relevance to us later when we come to discuss the difficulty of recognizing this factor of human uniqueness in generalized formulas that relate to learning, and especially in the evaluation of intelligence.

It follows from this that there is a much deeper and far more discreet strategy in the selection of an educational philosophy than in the saving of teachers' salaries. Students who learn less by guidance rely more upon the thinking strategies and experiences they came to school with to interpret and make sense of the generalized instruction and material that is presented to them. In turn, this means that the language ability of each student, to interpret and make use of the school material, will greatly depend upon the similarity or dissimilarity of this to their "homegrown" techniques and experiences. In effect, and in a general sense, this means that children are educated through a self-limiting environment, which traditionally ties each child to the world of their parents.

While it may be disconcerting to consider that the basic design of education was to make sure that citizens were raised to a certain degree of competence, we may gain some consolation in the knowledge that historically this had the purpose of guarding the operational efficiency of a working society. Mention of this draws us closer to examining how societies create and manufacture the level of intelligence they require in their members, as they seek to balance the design of their social operation against the technological level that supports their economic operation. To see the bigger picture in all this, it is to realise that the way the child processes information in school is much the way they will reason about information when they become a citizen.

We mentioned earlier the important distinction of a school child being promoted to the university level or being deprived of this and going either to college to be skilled or directly to a work role as unskilled. Our following chapter will go into more detail to explain why such distinction has always been important, and so why we must evolve out of this to create future citizens of more equal and higher reason.

Chapter Nine

The Modeling of Society Members

The basic purpose of a society is to operate with a sense of harmony. This requires efficient management from those in authority, and a trusting compliance from those who are managed. In the most direct sense, this is to say that the decisions for the lives of the citizens are made by those who govern them. When those in government work unselfishly and with pure honesty for this purpose, society may prosper to the benefit of all. History has shown us how seldom this occurs, and how the governing authority employs tactics (we may call this politics) to gain the greater acceptance of the people to support the designs it creates and seeks to manifest.

To this aim, the primary purpose of education lies in the management of the upcoming generation. It is to foster better skills in the ability of those who will come to manage, and to foster in those who are to be the managed a ready acceptance for information they will be presented with, and thereby governed through. As we discussed, education meets this purpose by dividing its operation into two tiers. Traditionally, these are the schools of general education and the universities.

Those who attend only the general education are taught to accept information as true and to respect the authority that gives it to them. Neither authority nor the information it provides is to be contested. Traditionally, information is to be studied by school children, but not challenged. As Kuhn reminds us, the student of general education is still: ".. rarely asked to take positions and develop arguments to justify them. Even less often must they coordinate the arguments and counterarguments entailed in skilled debate ...."[46] So, we find that school children are not taught fully how to understand what they are learning, and are largely judged on how well they have memorized the rules and content that is desired of them in their lessons.

While the general citizen is not taught how to think too much in their education, those who are to manage them must be. After all, those who make the decisions in government, society, and business are required to be more wary of information and to have a greater competence to challenge it for the higher levels of responsibility they are to have. It is for this reason that the undergraduate is taught skills of reason deprived to the student of general education.

May it then be understood that a university is not merely to provide its students with greater depths of information. It is to teach them how to challenge information by redefining and promoting all the skills that constitute the act of reason. The students of this tier are taught how to think.

So we find undergraduates today, learn not to write a brief essay on Aristotle's Rhetoric, but learn to make fine differentiation with Ethos (The ability to trust information on how credible its owner appears.),(How the perspectives of information change with its emotional appeal.), and Logos (How focus is given to the way reason is defined.) -- through numerous interactions of different and complex forms. So, as the university student makes their analysis of information, they can strengthen their reasoning by resorting to Norman's discourse to analyse the personality, politeness and sense of value behind the argument presented. All of this empowers them with qualities of reason and an awareness of how to better employ this, which is far above that of the student of general education.

It was Perry who produced a groundbreaking understanding of this education of reason way back in 1968, with his Perry Scheme. Perry identified a number of stages, from the virtual acceptance of information to a scientific inquiry into it. He explained how the role of the university is to transform the dualistic way of reasoning (developed at the general school level) to a higher and more adaptable level of reasoning. Perry termed this higher-level of reasoning, commitment to relativism or higher-level relativism.

While a number of terms have developed to explain these different levels of reasoning, I find it easier to use the term *evaluatist* for the undergraduate, as they come to evaluate different aspects of information to decide the greater worth of it.
Accordingly, the student of general education recognizes information as right or wrong, good or bad, with clear black and white distinctions. They would regard an assertion as being correct or incorrect as they perceive the situation, and would trust their teacher to provide them with knowledge that is correct and unquestionable. This *dualistic* thinker will see their purpose in school as being to remember and to reproduce the knowledge that is given to them from the authority of the teacher.

On the other hand, the undergraduate would be taught not to take information at its face value. They would be taught to reflect upon all points of view, and to reason the strength of validity of each. Consequently, they would be keen to engage the thoughts of others to test the validity of their own beliefs, and so develop to see the university lecturer as a conversation partner expressing an opinion.

This is different from the school child who is coached to see their teacher as having infallible authority. Thus, the undergraduate is taught to learn information through skills of debate,[47] and so evolves a higher level of information management than the school child. Through the experiences they engage, the undergraduate gains proficiency in organizing their thinking processes.

We see here that as each student moves through education and into society, they prepare the ground for their children who will follow them, by the skills of reason they gained or did not. We have been raised by a social consciousness to believe that children are different in their intelligence in school because they inherit different qualities of this. Yet, we can see here how intelligence is engineered by design to be socially transmitted.

In essence, we may say that the parent who has been to university has been taught higher skills to interact with their world and they will naturally transmit these to their child, while the parent who was deprived of this awareness will not know how they are not developing their child!

In the 19th century, this stratification of opportunity to education and so work and social rank was very clear. It became less so in the 20th century, as changes in society forced changes in education that forced it to be less selective and to appear to be more egalitarian.

- In consequence of this socio-educational architecture, a minority of students will acquire education in their skills of reason that the larger number of their generation will be deprived of. The threshold level that decides the ratio of this division (i.e, what percentage of students will enter university to acquire these higher reasoning skills) is essentially determined by the level of the technology of the society.

So, we find, for example, that in the technological level of 1926, only eight students in every 10,000 of the British population were required to have a university education to oversee all governmental and industrial decisions.[48] This ratio changed drastically as technology advanced and brought demand from employers for higher proficiency in reasoning ability. By 1961, with the advent of deep changes in work and society, one school child in every 18 then went on into higher education.

Twenty years later, as we engaged the computerized era, one child in every eight went beyond their generalized education to be skilled in higher forms of thinking.[49] To bring this in line with our own times, we may be reminded of President Obama predicting that nearly 50% of all jobs will require levels of reason beyond a high school education by 2020.[50] This is to say that in theory, one in every two school students will be required to go to university. This, of course, brings many problems to the university, because the school can not bring such a level of its students up to the standard of the university as we have seen.

It is relevant to note that while the higher education of today (encompassing university, college, and further education courses) does not accomplish the same development of reasoning as the traditional university, those who leave school without this opportunity may be more likely to evaluate information on its apparent strength.

All of this means that while society traditionally requires education to produce citizens of basically two levels of reasoning, the technology of today has disturbed and must continue to disturb the historical purpose of this. As we may now understand, this division of reasoning skills (which is really intelligence) has always been a criterion of civilisation, because it facilitated better cooperation and government of people.

In the simplest sense, this management of reason created within those deprived of an opportunity to develop themselves better, a sense of inferiority and so dependency, both of which made them more willing to comply and conform.

Before the 1970s, this division was largely based on and justified through wealth, since wealth was traditionally related to ownership of land and this to governing responsibility. As wealthy parents could afford a better quality of education for their child (smaller classes and a better learning environment), and were able to employ direct and indirect means to get them into university, they were able to provide an education of reason that would secure a better future for them. Those parents who were not so able were provided with a lower level of education for their children. In this way, the status quo was not only held but also conveyed through generations.

Since education had been oriented towards opportunity and wealth, it was the private schools that traditionally supplied students for university, while the state schools fed the general working needs of the society. Impression arose through this that students entering university did so because they came from better genetic stock. However, it is to be realized that the opportunities for children in the private and the state schools were very, very different.

One essential difference then, as now, lay not so much in the quality of the teacher, although better teachers were attracted to better schools, but in the means by which the teacher was able to involve themselves in the personal development of each child in their class. In this way, private education provided not only a more enlightened atmosphere, but it also gave each student far more guidance to understand what they were being taught by their teachers. Accordingly, the child whose parents paid for their education obtained far more from their teachers in extra time, extra lessons, and a holistic atmosphere that was geared through competition to their academic success. This was not so for the child who attended a state school and left at half past three to return to a home of social distractions.

Another crucial difference between private and state education often lies in the size of the class. While a private school sought to give the teacher smaller classes, by which they could interact closely with each student, state schools normally had larger classes. This compounded the difficulties for the student in the state school to gain a quality of understanding, since their teacher would struggle through far more disassociated minds than in the private school to explain the lesson content.

We may understand from this that, in general, the minds of children in the state school came from homes where mental discipline was lacking, stimulation was vague, interest was simply satisfied, and all were driven by a different sense of purpose than those of the private school.[51] The student in the state school, may it be said, would be much left to their own resources to survive, despite the efforts and ability of their teachers. At the end of the day, the only thing witnessed was that children from wealthier backgrounds obtained better results in school, with the cause obviously implied when all factors of social inheritance and related opportunities were played down.

The contention with education, we may now understand, was in the way it selected children for university, and so the right to greater opportunity in society. Traditionally, education controlled this right through the wealth of the child's family. However, as technology advanced and more capable "managers" were required, education was increasingly pressurized to sponsor bright children from poor backgrounds who could not otherwise afford this opportunity.

While such sponsoring had to be necessarily limited, to maintain the required ratio of backgrounds to opportunity, society had to implement strategies that would limit the ability of children in education to maintain the stability it required for its operations.

We need not to lose hold of the manager/managed and so evaluatist/dualistic thinker purpose of education, which has always been a disguised mandate for it.

While many of the more obvious strategies behind this no longer exist, the subtlest of them still do. Fisher found that many societies purposely create social policies that hinder the intellectual development of children who belong to a politically undesired group. He found evidence of this with Catholics in Northern Ireland, Koreans in Japan, and Sephardic Jews in Israel.[52]

While the development of a certain group of children can be politically managed against their interests and so future opportunities, the process of assessment within education can give fine tune to this discrimination. This, of course, can occur at the individual level. Many parents, it may be noted, have too often explained to me that they dare not complain about the way their child is being taught, in fear that the teacher in question would deliberately under mark their child. This is a very real concern, and one I know can be well justified. However, just as the process of assessment can be used against an individual or a group of politically undesired children, I found it astonishing to come across a case where it was used to create gender inequality in England in the 1990s.

To mention this brings us to discuss the case of a young woman named Alex. I first met Alex while purchasing something in a shop. We spoke briefly and introduced ourselves. "My name is Alex." She said. I queried her, as if she meant to say Alessandra. "No!" She told me. She was christened with the name Alex. Seeing the slight puzzlement on my face, Alex explained that at the time of her birth, her mother had read an article about how a local school had been discovered deliberately lowering the scores of girls in their school work and examinations. This, it was discussed, artificially raised the scores of boys, with a view to giving males more opportunities than females in the future generation. It was to prevent her daughter from being so discriminated against that the mother gave her a name that could be used by a girl but was seen in a register as that of a boy.

It arises from this that with such thinking, tactics can be engineered through the design of educational material and means of assessment at the national level to pre-select children. As we have mentioned, while the material and the methodology of teaching appear to present equal opportunity, it can be presented through a language that biases opportunity.

To understand how education works through language, it is necessary to realise that through their home background, each child will have their own skills of language by which their world can be understood. As meanings, intentions, and descriptions circulate within a community, the children of one community can develop a different working language from that of children of another community.

Since communities are divided into economic status, children from wealthier neighborhoods have a different language than children from poorer neighborhoods. This is not a one or the other situation, but it does allow education to select on a national basis one quality of language to use for all its students. This language can improve or hinder the opportunities of children, according to their background.

Much of how this operated came to light late in the 20th century, as socio-pathological discussions arose to examine cases of cultural deprivation.[53] This was further understood through teaching practices, which were developed to teach children through their own socio-cultural language.

For example, it was realized that the English minds of African-American students differed from the English minds of white American students because of cultural differences. This did cause them difficulty to learn and progressing at an equal rate to white children in their education. Knowledge of this language difficulty in their education gave rise to a language system that is specifically designed to help African-American children overcome this problem. Ebonics does this with very successful results, as it emphasizes the significance of language in school, in grades, and so in the development of intelligence.[54/55/56]

When educational material is insensitive to the language of children's minds, or designed against the languages of some in favor of those of others, it causes some children a difficulty that other children do not have as they learn. Consider the cryptic question:

Question: Fellow departs to produce fruit?
Answer: Mango. (as in man goes)

All children who know English will know each of the words in the question: fellow, depart, produce, and fruit, but to make sense of the order in which they are presented here requires a developed skill. Therefore, to be able to answer this question requires familiarity with its style of language. Without such familiarity, the question is quite indecipherable. With it, it is relatively easy.

Language, then, in an educational context, relates to the fluid awareness and management of words, which can be tied to a cultural or social base and not just to the size of the vocabulary. We may recall in *The Dead Poets Society*, the first thing that Robin Williams did when he started his new class was to instruct the pupils to rip out the first few pages of one of their textbooks. He did this because the style of language used was confusing for them. This, we can suggest, was to demonstrate (to viewers) the need to change the style of language in education, to make textbooks easier for a wider range of children to understand.

It is, then, of great significance to us to know that a student's unfamiliarity with the language of their education does not reflect their intelligence. It only demonstrates that they do not understand the way information is presented to them and how they should respond to it.

While this design works on a national basis, on a local basis, the pre-selection of children can be devised through the quality of schooling. We find, for instance, that when "School districts rely heavily on property taxes for their funding, (*this* means that schools in affluent areas get more money than those in middle and poor ones. Tax money to fill the void fails to make ends meet in school districts where poverty levels are greatest."[57]

Better areas in a community, therefore, tend to produce better schools. They entice the more competent teachers, and are largely more able to support a higher general level of quality through the support of wealthier parents. These parents are very likely to raise extra funds for the school, and just as likely to entice local political directives to support their aim. Tyack drew reference to this in America, where he recorded the instruction given by a superintendent to his staff advising them that: "Here on the hill, in a wealthy suburban district, is a grammar school, its organisation, administration and course of study must necessarily differ from that other school, located in the heart of the factory district."[58]

This illustration is relevant today in many countries, as it reveals a purpose to limit children to their background opportunities. I find that schools in developed countries try to hide this distinction, while schools in underdeveloped countries openly play upon it. Nevertheless, we can see in this a clear suggestion of the kind of pressures that can be placed on a child who enters a better educational stream, but who comes from the wrong background. Either they adapt the "right profile," or they leave.[59] Privileged schools can be found in most countries today, irrespective of their politics, where they seek to secure the future of their selected children through the exclusion of other children and base their claim to elitism on the concept of inherited ability.

The old political idea in society of the child inheriting the brains of their parents is what gave acceptance to Thorndike's theories of how children learn and should be taught in education. Accordingly, Thorndike's system taught children in large masses in very conditioning environments, so there was very little opportunity for the student to develop their skills of interaction. So, while stability in performance was said to be caused by an inherited quality of intelligence, it was actually caused by such a highly conditioning and self-limiting environment!

Chapter Ten

The Evolvement of Education

As education was developing in early 20th-century America, as it did in virtually all countries at that time, great emphasis was placed on the child's inherited ability and very little on how they could develop in learning. It was much in reaction to this that Watson, as we saw in stating that any child could be raised to do any job, was driven to bring greater awareness to the value of the environment.

To emphasize to teachers the significance of the environment in learning, Watson devised a formula that showed the relationship between the child and their learning. The formula itself is very simple.

In fact, it is too simple. Yet, it did give people something they could instantly relate to, understand, and hold on to. It was through this reasoning that Watson was able to bring some degree of balance to the expounded belief of inherited ability. This now famous "S-R" formula states that it is the Stimulus (or information) that produces the Response (the answer) a child gives. In other words, the better informed the child is, the better their answer will be.

As we may imagine, this Stimulus to Response formula for learning did not endear itself to the categorizing principles of a cost conscious educational service. Accordingly, it was not readily accepted into teaching principles. The main objection, of course, was that it advocated the idea that response was decided purely by stimuli. Education had a vested interest in not promoting this idea for all the reasons we have discussed, because it purposely ignored any effect of inheritance. Teachers in the classroom may have heard of Watson's idea, but the system under which they worked gave them little opportunity to put it into practice.

However, largely through Watson's efforts, the role of the environment in learning did become more accepted by some educationalists, and this helped to stoke the argument as to which was more important in intelligence, "Was it the inherited aspect or was it the developed?" This had long since been referred to as the Nature-Nurture argument, but it still persists to this day. In "Intelligence: The Great Lie," we shall make a close examination of this. Yet, in the 1930s, a psychologist by the name of Skinner blended the worth of the child into Watson's S-R formula.

Skinner's S-O-R formula[60] states that any Response to Stimulus (information) is dependent upon the Organism's (or the student's) ability. To different people, this meant different things. To those who wanted to promote the use of the environment, the role of the Organism was taken to mean motivation. In fact, this formula was not originally Skinner's. He only adopted it from Robert Woodworth, who had devised it to explain the use of motivation.[61] However, to the greater number of those who followed the belief in inherited ability, and so decided the way education worked, the Organism gave proof that the response of the individual was dependent upon their genetic limitation. With this reasoning, no dramatic effect was noticed in teaching and evaluation practices, save a more general acceptance to the effect of the environment.

- Accordingly, the general education of children went on much as before, as did assessment of their potential. It needs to be realized, and it seldom is, that while educationalists often refer to Watson's S-R formula and Skinner's S-O-R formula to explain how children are taught, these formulas were only theoretical explanations. How children actually learned, how they were actually taught, and how they were so examined had nothing to do with these.

Throughout the time of Watson and Skinner, nothing changed in the way students were taught and assessed in education. Classes were filled with large numbers of students, who sat at respectable distances away from the teacher and the scribbling they made on the blackboard. They were told to learn from pages 40 to 45 in their textbooks, and they were periodically examined on their competence to understand what the teacher was supposed to have explained to them. In fact, nothing really changed in education from the 1800s until Jean Piaget arrived in the 1960s. So, whatever we shall come to say about his concepts, it must always be realized that it was directly because of Piaget that a pivotal change for the better was brought into the whole school experience.

Therefore, it was only children in areas of special learning who benefited through practical applications of first Watson's and then Skinner's theories, as means were sought to help them to overcome their learning problems. The funding for this was raised not so much to enable these children to have a better life, but to provide extra assistance to enable them to develop to be relatively dependable workers. This will become very clear when we discuss in *Intelligence* why the French government employed Binėt, and so how the concept of how to measure intelligence first arose.

In the decade after the Second World War, the whole structure of civilisation began to change. Compounded by the development of technology that evolved out of this war, and so the work and social shifts that came to the surface because of it, education became ever more egalitarian. This brought demand for a serious improvement in the capability of students, and alternative methods of education began to be sought. As we have seen, it was these demands that forced education to replace the old idea of "work by exercise" with thoughts of how children learn, and could learn better. The ideal candidate to provide direction for this was the Swiss psychologist Jean Piaget.

Although Piaget had developed his philosophy of how children learn in the 1920s and had been widely accepted in psychological circles, his philosophy was not generally embraced by education until these turbulent times demanded radical changes.[62] There were two reasons for his acceptance:

Firstly, Piaget had reasoned that children mature in biological stages, with parallel stages of increasing levels of intellectual understanding. These biological stages broadly coincided with how the school system was organized, so that education could easily assimilate his philosophy into its design. For example, by his 2nd stage (2 to 7 years), children attended nursery school. At the 3rd stage (7 to 11 years), children attended their primary education, and at the beginning of the 4th stage (11 years to adulthood) they entered high school.[63]

Secondly, Jean Piaget's philosophy centered around the idea that children adapt better to their environment when they learn by themselves. Piaget was trying to get away from the too often overbearing and instructor-like teacher, who was the product of Thorndike's philosophy. This kind of disciplinarian too often frightened their students, and in doing so actually inhibited their ability to learn.

The idea that children learn best by themselves provided a political ideology that education was looking for. This enabled education to say that children were now focusing on the environment in their learning, which appeased the increasing demands from left-wing elements in education.

However, what was little realized is that Piaget's philosophy much more supported the right-wing element's need for social stratification, which it based on inherited ability. This was provided through the very strong biological foundation of Piaget's developmental stages, and the act by which a student was caused to learn by themselves.

When the teacher was inhibited from teaching, as teachers were through fear of interfering in the child's personal interaction, the child was purposely left to their home-based skills to understand. In real terms, this meant that the child self-conditioned their perspective of what they were doing and so self-limited their development. Without a source of mediation to overcome this, the performance of children remained stable, and the concept of inherited ability varying about the average was retained, albeit under a more exciting and acceptable guise in those increasingly sensitive political times. Fueled now by Piaget's comment to create active individuals capable of doing new things,[64] education moved into the new era of self-activation.

It is interesting to note here that while Thorndike had based his theories on how children learn on a biological framework, from his observation of rats, Piaget, at heart a biologist, did no less. Piaget developed his theories of how children adapt to learn through studies of the water snail Limnaea stagnalis. As this snail alters the shape of its shell to survive in different environments, Piaget based his philosophy on the same principle to explain how children develop their understanding through fixed biological stages.[65] Reasoning developed through this that as the snail changes its shell by recognition of a new environment, so children adapt and learn by their need to do so. This was taken to mean that the teacher interferes with this natural process of adaptation. As Piaget's theory that children adapt to learn became broadly interpreted to mean that children learn best by themselves, a whole new design was brought into education, the effects of which soon became obvious.

Since education could now argue that children can learn by themselves, the need for teachers, as well as the cost of employing them, was reduced. In effect, this gave education an excuse to increase the number of children in the classroom, which, with the atmosphere of discipline now removed, soon became a free-for-all. In turn, this increasing chaos further impacted the ability of the teacher to guide their students with a reasonable quality of understanding. The lower value of teaching that came out of this caused students to learn less, even though they were given more stimulus. So, as one cancelled out the other, the performance of students in their lessons remained stable. This enabled education to continue to define their ability in accordance with the design placed upon it.

While education was struggling to justify how students could take written examinations (for the education they had largely devised by themselves through open-ended learning and project assessments), it was suddenly confronted with a major stumbling block.

As technological advancements in the 1970s began to demand that education produce more adaptable and responsible workers, the speed at which they occurred placed such pressure on employers that they could not afford to wait for education to provide them with such greater competence. In their need to be competitive, they brought about a new concept in education; that of adult education.

Much of the demand for this had been brought out through the global success of Japanese products, as developed through the ideas of the American business consultant W.E.Deming. It was Deming's revolutionary philosophies in production, service, and management training that began to transform the concept of work ideology, and with it the role of the worker and the relevance of their competence.[66/67]

As competence became more of a determinable quality in the worker, it brought pressure on education to devise a more competent educational system, which it now saw to lie in greater environmental awareness. This brought fresh interest to follow Montessori's lead in making the classroom environment more natural and enjoyable,[68] and then by the keener interest this stimulated to resurface the philosophies of the 18th-century French educationalist Jean-Jacques Rousseau. Rousseau had strongly advocated the idea of natural learning. He believed that if a child were placed in the right environment, they would flourish as would a plant. Put them in the wrong environment and they will dry up and perish! This naturalistic philosophy brought out a greater desire to let the child learn by their own achievements, which was in tune with Piaget's philosophy.

However, as the classroom environment became less structured, studies by other psychologists of the ways in which children learn began to question the way they looked at the world, rather than the way we looked at it through their responses. In consequence to this, ideas began to arise that children were not limited in their response by the rigidity of the biological stages suggested by Piaget, but by the language of their world and their relative inexperience and insecurities.[69]

Although the Russian neurologist Alexander Luria had explained how mental development is related to language experience in the 1930s,[70] and shared Vygotsky's reasoning, it was not until Noam Chomsky suggested we gain language ability by adapting the environment to innate schemas thirty years later[71] that education began to look at how language decides learning. This brought greater questions about how intelligence could be decided by the environment.

As Chomsky reasoned that thought was a consequence of language, he brought focus on social tactics in learning. It was much through this that the question began to arise on the validity of Piaget's belief that language, and so intelligence, was a consequence of phases of biological development. As this became more questioned, contention began to grow that these stages, as the far-reaching consequences of them in education and social spheres, were actually based on children responding to what they believed was expected of them, rather than what they were capable of doing![72]

For example, Piaget's theme was based on the development of a child's motor activity, which he saw as having parallels with their mental activity. On these lines, Piaget argued that a child between the ages of 11 and 15 could do mental tasks that a child between the ages of 7 and 11 could not do. However, this perspective of the strict relationship between motor competence and mental conceptions does not hold. They are of different functions of the body, and although they support each other, the design of their development has different bases. For example, by 2 years of age, we have grown to some 20% of what we may reach in maturity, yet our brain weight at this stage is 80% of its mature value.

We may add to this that by measuring the rate of glucose metabolism in the brain, Chugani has shown that between the ages of 2 and 4, our brain absorbs information faster than at any other time in our lives.[73] Yet at this time, we are only beginning to develop our muscular ability.

It also needs to be pointed out that 11 years of age (Piaget's 4th stage) can be the beginning of puberty, and that children change in their perspective of learning at this time, because they become more defensive of their own values.

As more studies began to examine the performance of individual children, Piaget's definition of what a child could mentally do at any one time was found not to be consistent with his idea of abrupt pattern changes. Instead, it became realized that any indexing of ability was relatable to the emotional character of the child, and to the socio-cultural developmental path they moved through.[74] Thus, development became recognizable through the holistic experience that was related to the child, rather than to their biological process unfolding!

Accordingly, Piaget's idea that an infant cannot recognise hidden objects until they have reached a certain age (i.e., 12 months), suggests that this is a biological developmental stage and so open to genetic ability. However, Sophian showed the ability of an infant to recognise or fail to recognise hidden objects at this age is simply reliant upon the practice they have had in retaining information.[75]

We may add to this that within the first year of life, the infant is attracted to focus upon singular events to the exclusion of others, because they need to learn from singular experiences how to relate to multiple ones. This task is simply coincidental of their age development. Similar arguments can be given to explain each of the developmental stages Piaget defined, so that instead of seeing what is thought to be the unfolding of a genetic development, we are really only identifying with a developmental condition. As greater question arose as to what developmental stages could actually mean, the use of education to regard the different aptitudes of different children at the same developmental age became more questionable.

As brain scanning and brain imaging techniques became more advanced in the 1980s, they enabled neuroscientists to gain a higher understanding of how the brain could be shaped by environmental interaction. Although this is a discussion for *"Brain Plasticity,"* we may understand here that this knowledge opened up a whole new ideology in education, which took the fashionable term of "brain learning."[76]

As "brain learning" gave educationalists something new to work with, it opened up ideas that a student's ability to understand information is more dependent upon how they interact with it than Piaget had reasoned. In turn, this drew attention to the quality of guidance the student received as they developed. Taking the lead that Chomsky had provided with language, education sought to transcend itself from Piaget's self-adaptation to ideas of greater environmental adaptation.

Yet, this transcendence was not clear-cut, because while newer teachers listened to new ideas, they often found themselves operating from textbooks and work schedules that were for a long time Piagetian in theme. Partly in an effort to improve the child's access to the environment, and partly to support the suggestions of "brain learning," educationalists began to reason that children should be unbound in how they interacted with information, and yet taught how to think more about what they were doing.

This set off ideas that children could learn through the creation and organisation of their own projects, while experiencing a much watered-down version of the kind of epistemological reasoning that was reserved for the university level. By this means, the concept of critical thinking became phased into the self-exploration that students were now doing. This, at least, was the theory.

In a traditional education, the assessment of student progress is determined through tests and examinations, based on the textbooks they use. However, once education allowed students to devise their own projects and style of learning, these tests were no longer appropriate. It was in trying to evaluate how well students were progressing towards their final examinations, in the level of disorder that project work had created in the classroom, that caused education to replace class tests with teacher assessments. However, the university still demanded formal examinations they could trust, so final examinations were retained to evaluate ability in the final stages of the child's school career.

As assessments replaced class tests, it was realized that this move deprived students of the psychological and history of experience to deal with their final examinations, which the testing process had prepared them for. Basically, tests are an integral part of the learning process. Class tests force students to review information frequently, so they are caused to be more familiar with it and less likely to forget it. Most importantly, class tests give an opportunity to re-encounter what was previously misunderstood. When students are forced to constantly reassess information, they are caused to realise a higher understanding of what they have done. This generates higher qualities of recognition, which better arm them for the problem-solving tasks of their examinations.

Deprived of this level of experience, and the psychological experience of preparing and dealing with the exam situation, students began to demonstrate such levels of stress that education was induced to replace its final examinations with coordinated assessments -- as much as the university would allow.

Yet, the evaluation of an assessment is not as straightforward as the marking of a test. Under test conditions, the student is forced to demonstrate their worth, but assessments enable them to copy from others, so that the effort they present is seldom their own. This can distort what the individual may actually be capable of, and draws the personal relationship of the student into the teacher's assessment of their work in a way that is avoided with tests. Therefore, the parameters by which an assessment is derived are very different from those by which a test is judged.

Without the strict guidelines under which a teacher may mark a test paper, the marking of an assessment is more open to different evaluation by different teachers. As an example, it may be said that if a student were to submit a test paper to three different teachers in three different schools, each should determine it worthy of, say, a grade of 8. However, if the same student were to be assessed in three different schools, then it is likely they would obtain different grades from the different teachers. One teacher may award an 8, another a 10, and the third possibly a 6. Education strives to overcome such disparity. Yet, as this is an inherent reality of assessment marking, it does extend an indisputable unreliability to a student's profile, as much as it does to the profile of the whole educational system.

To society at large, the variability that assessments bring to the evaluation of the student is hidden by the variability of the overall educational system. It has, after all, nothing else to relate it to, save an impression that earlier generations of school pupils were more competent. This means that while examinations show exactly what the student is worth, they also show exactly the worth of their education. Assessments, on the other hand, enable education to hide how effective it has been in the development of the student. As we have seen, the teacher decides what they want to decide when they grade the student, and they do this in accordance with the expectations of their system.

Therefore, while tests and examinations gave a reliable indication of the constructive worth of an educational system, assessments offer too little real understanding of its effectiveness. Yet, to the machinery of education, it enables the teacher ease in modifying pupil differences about the average, which is expected of them. In turn, this enables education to retain control over the whole learning, developmental, and evaluation process, and make it appear to be more effective than it is. Dewey brought awareness to this when he wrote:

"It is easy to fall into the habit of regarding the mechanics of school organization and administration as something comparatively external and indifferent to educational purposes and ideals. We forget that it is such matters as the classifying of pupils, the way decisions are made, and the manner in which the machinery of instruction bears upon the child that really controls the whole system."[77]

The disparity of assessments is of much concern to the university, because it has to determine the capability of a prospective undergraduate to complete their course of study. In recognition of this, different educational systems seek to appease the demands of their universities in different ways. Some have retained written paper examinations, such as the SAT in America, while other countries present an ability-based system based on progressive assessments and examinations. Others, such as Denmark, evaluate ability with both written and verbal assessments.

This generalized account of the development of education is only a flavor of what took place in most countries, because each would have tackled these situations under their own stresses and strains. Yet, it does bring relevance to allow us to understand where education came from and where it is today. The question we must now ask ourselves is, "How will it progress in the future?"

Chapter Eleven

Education: From What and To Where

"Education is shaped by political policies that arise through social changes. These often evolve out of technological developments. Yet, by the time education has adapted to these changes, they are usually out of date. Today, education risks being out of date when it focuses upon computerization, without considering and preparing for the deep social changes this could bring."

Roy Andersen

So, we saw how the initial design of a general education employed a single teacher to instruct 50 or 60 children in a class, although it could be many more, who were to learn more by repetition than understanding. We saw that this highly economical system could only be justified with the belief that the intelligence of the student was largely inherited. This provided the ideal argument for education, for when it could be said the child obtained their grade much as a consequence of their natural ability, education had an excuse for its failure in not providing a better learning environment.

Yet, in reality, it was the environment that the school created that determined how the child progressed in their education. Those who were more familiar with that environment and more stimulated through their home environment did better and so scored higher in examinations. Those who could relate less to school, and for whatever reason were more distracted or troubled, scored less. Whatever view was held of the use of the environment, at the end of their education the grade the child gained, and so the role they would take in society was said to be more or less determined by what they were born with.

As an understanding that the quality of the environment had something to do with this ability, class sizes became reduced to 30 or so children to allow the teacher to maximize on this new concept. Yet, what the environment actually meant to the individual child in their lessons was never realized in practice.

In our necessarily short appraisal of Piaget, we have focused upon how education made use of his biological perspective of how children learn. However, it must be realized that it was primarily through Piaget that education evolved out of and away from the strict world of instruction that demanded children copy the information dictated to them. It was, we must recognise, totally through the humanitarian efforts of this great man that the child in school took their learning less from textbooks, which too often were written by adults for adults, into a hands-on experience.

It was this move that caused the child to do better in their learning, because they could now better associate to what was happening. As it was gradually realized that children learned better by themselves than from an often intimidating, if not frightening, disciplinarian, the form of their learning began to change. In the beginning, they were allowed to learn through their own assignments. This prompted the idea that they should work in groups and so develop through each other by sharing thoughts. In turn, this brought the suggestion that children should be taught ideas of critical thinking to enable them to better understand this learning process.

All of this may have been in vogue with Piaget's thinking, but as the administrators in education saw the instructor to fade out of the learning experience, they caused the presence of the teacher to move further into the background. The idea now was that children learn best by themselves, and the teacher was not to interfere in this. Once this view of their role was taken, the teacher became more of an observer and so judge of the child's ability, rather than a teacher directly participating in the personal evolution of each child's learning experience. However, this now meant that the only way the child could understand and so perform lay in the ways they had been taught at home, because they were now deprived of close guidance from the teacher.

With too little knowledge and too much ignorance of what this home development meant in intelligence, it was taken as confirmation of a biological inheritance. In other words, the inherited aspect of intelligence was retained. May we see here that by adopting Piaget's philosophy, education was able to show how children learn better through greater environmental interaction, while at the same time grounding their learning and the assessments made of them to its traditional belief of inherited ability. The basic operation of education did not change!

We have yet to discuss Vygotsky, but Vygotsky offered an alternative means of educating children to that offered by Piaget. While Piaget had transformed the disciplinarian teacher who taught by instruction to a passive teacher who observed children learning through their own efforts, Vygotsky sought to create a teacher who explained knowledge in the language of the child, to the relevance of their experiences. To explain this, he developed the concept of the Zone of Proximal Development.

Vygotsky's Zone of Proximal Development, or ZPD, lies between what the child knows and what they do not know.

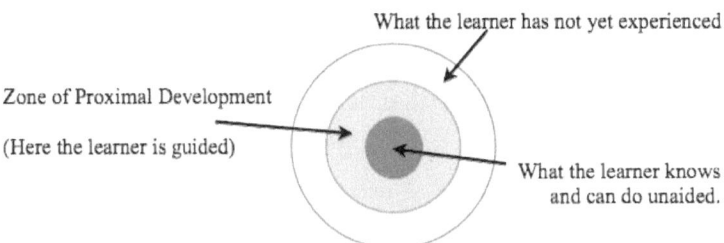

In essence, this is the basic principle of mediation, and for future references, and there will be many in our books, we should hold in mind this simple illustration of the Zone of Proximal Development. Mediation, we are to discuss, is where the more experienced guide the less experienced from what they know to what they do not know. Yet, it is important to realise that mediation, as any form of teaching or guidance, is only given value through a clear understanding of what "The Art of Sensitivity in Awareness" means.

More simply in this example of the zone of proximal development, it would not be to think of a particular zone but to consider a number of levels within each zone. Thus, if in each zone the teacher discusses with the student what they think they know and having improved this for them, what they expect to encounter as they further develop, they will cause them to be more sensitive in their handling of information.

With this higher awareness, the student will be more able to predict what is expected of them and so be less likely to import ideas which are not relevant, which they do when they don't understand what they are doing. It is by the constant dialogue of how the student understands their past understanding, how they see the way information is presented at this moment, and how they could predict what may happen next, is the means by which the teacher would significantly develop their ability and with this the confidence that arms them to explore and self-correct as they develop this.

However, the problem is that Vygotsky's idea, just as those of every other educationalist before and after him, seeks to improve learning for the individual student, but students do not learn individually. They learn amongst a mass of confused personalities who strive with different interests to be in the class or try to avoid being in it, often guided by a teacher who is pressurized simply to give information, mark the responses they get, and move to the next lesson, with a few moments here and there for the most problematic in the class.

It was through this understanding, I realized the importance of the attitude of the teacher and how this directs the attitude of the students, and from which I put forward a philosophy in teaching and learning encapsulated by the term "The Andersen Attitude Method of Teaching"

All the above aspects we have just mentioned are ones we shall come back to in time. However, in the development of education, Vygotsky's philosophy was not known outside of Russia until the 1960s, and although there were many educationalists in the West who had similar ideas to his, they were seldom given the means to make practical use of them in the classroom.

So, in nearly two centuries, there have been great changes in the school experience for the child. Plastic chairs and communal tables have replaced wooden pews and benches, which has made the environment more homely, which seemingly encourages children to interact more with it. The language of education in textbooks and examinations that once clearly defined the opportunities or limitations to each child, as they were familiar with this, has changed to present greater and fairer parity to all. With an ever-increasing realization of the true role of the environment, information became more colorful, imaginative, and more manageable, which did improve the opportunity of each child to do better.

However, as we have just shown, the deeper changes that would have released the child from the mechanism of a stratified future remain a controlled process, for the need of and the machinery which desired discrimination has not altered. It has merely changed its appearance to survive. The grade the child gains is still set about the conditioned average and still regarded as a mixture of their motivation and inherited quality, with the competence of the teacher, and so education is little brought into the equation. In all this, the teacher has long been phased into the background, and so deprived of the opportunity to interact and improve each child's progression of their understanding; without which the child struggles to survive among 30 or so other children blinkered by their personal understanding of why, how, when, and what they should do as assessment of their competence is ever more refined.

With these words, we are brought up-to-date in our understanding of how education has evolved from what it began as to what it is at this moment. From this point, we move to consider how education could develop in the future. This is a future that suggests radical changes in the whole concept of the design of education, and yet there is too little awareness of this by educationalists.

Chapter Twelve
Digital Interference

As we entered this new century, education saw itself ever more adapted to the presence of computers and the world of IT, which is influencing the design of the working world to which it is responsible.

So, we find that moves are developing to provide each student with their own computer in the classroom. The curriculum has now been altered in many countries to teach computer programming skills to children as young as five years of age,[78] and a whole movement is seeping through education, intent on changing its traditional role as information becomes increasingly digital. This is a move that in some future time may well lead to the human teacher being replaced by an electronic one, and children assessed on their keyboard skills. If the latter does occur, it will evoke a level of human classification on a par with the IQ testing of the 1920s in America, which was based on the belief that intelligence was essentially inherited.

It is now of some considerable relevance to know that the educational system in Denmark has relied upon computer software for the past seven years to test and evaluate its students in certain subjects. This system was thought to be exemplary, until it was realized in 2015 that the program was underevaluating student worth. In cases in which students were presented with 10 questions to answer for a text, but found themselves with only time to answer, for example, 8, the program erased the questions that had not been answered in believing the total had been completed. In effect, this meant that some students were receiving grades in their final examinations that were one or two grades below those they should have received. As a direct consequence of this, the educational system in Denmark has withdrawn computers from examinations and now requires its students to answer their questions with pen and paper.[79]

Setting this example aside, since it is to be assumed that programmers will seek to rectify the image this error has given to them, it is probable that education globally will evolve into a computer-driven institution. If it does so, it will fail to be out of date with the shifting requirements of society, as it always has been.

At the close of the last century, we realized the need for students to be more computer literate, but the development of artificial intelligence and the digital era since then suggests a change in the purpose of the citizen, and so the ways they are to be educated. This is because developments, such as those emerging through nanotechnology, could well force cataclysmic changes in our social design, and this would necessitate the citizen to have very high interpersonal skills, which the solitary experience of a computer-driven education would deprive them of.

Computers are so much a part of our world now that it is imperative that all children learn a great proficiency in working with them. However, there is a great danger in allowing computers to take over traditional handwriting skills and the familiarity we gain with a book when we turn its pages. To hold a pen to paper and transcribe letters in a beautiful fashion is an art we no longer teach. Yet, in all aspects of learning it is sensitivity that counts, and it is awareness to this value that we must hold on to.

- The whole process of learning is reliant upon sensitivity, and sensitivity is reliant upon intention, overcoming distraction. Pen and paper skills inspire this intention.

To be aware of controlling a pen to markedly distinguish between "o" and "u", and between "i" and "e" does have real meaning for clarity and usage in spelling. We have discussed the whole grammatical process, where one child presents their thoughts to another. However, it is not just thoughts that are presented, because thoughts hinge upon desires and feelings, and this is what we must learn to communicate more.

Computers are a wonderful source of information. With the swipe of a finger over a trackpad and a light tap, more information can be instantly available than having to plod through a book for an hour. While this has obvious advantages in searching for specific information, it raises caution that children are developing to judge information with a vagueness that lowers the sensitivity that develops precision in thinking. It also highlights the fact that in their scan and select process, the student can come to readily accept the authenticity of what they have found. As they scan, acknowledge, scan, and acknowledge, they develop to be trusting of information, and we have spent a few pages discussing what this means.

This "easy to find" facility encourages students to skip reading a book to find the information they need. Yet, in doing this, they can fail to be aware of other perspectives on the value of that information. When this happens, the student fails to grasp the meaning of the whole picture, which is what this learning task is trying to teach them. This takes us back to children developing to see school as a place where they give the fastest answer without understanding why they give it.

Computers emphasize what can go wrong with education. When students are encouraged to use a computer to compile their answer to a task, they can give a false impression of what they have really achieved. Thus, they can search through Google to find, select, and paste information into a report without knowing anything about the subject matter. Accordingly, the student produces a good report and will gain a good mark, without knowing very much about the information in that report.

So, the teacher gives an assignment, the student complies, is evaluated, and as one step follows another, education can show how the student performs. However, once they leave this magical kingdom and enter the real world, employers wonder why they cannot write a decent letter and why this new employee thinks eggs come from wheat.

The point being that it is not the quality of the answer the student provides that is what is really sought by the evaluation, but how much of that answer they really understand. As we have mentioned, knowing something and being able to explain it to another are not the same thing. The latter can be more easily corrected once the former has been, but not the other way around.

Computers create an educational system where students submit their assignments and may gain full marks for doing so. The student is happy with this, as are their parents, and so the educational system is evaluated and processed. However, if a parent demanded that the child verbally explain the answer they gave, it would be disillusioning for all. Not only may the child not know what they were evaluated on, but in learning through a computer, they would have poor language skills to explain their thoughts. The need for education in the future will be to develop the language skills of its students to enable them to be active with the democratic voice.

Reading a book gives a depth of understanding to information that computers often fail to do, which stimulates imagination and, through this, intelligence, which incidentally is one of the reasons why I wrote the romantic adventure "Whisperings of Betrayal." Thus, a book can also provide a more trustworthy source of information to the student in the context of the task they are given. However, the book offers other experiences too. To turn a page is a conscious action that makes the brain aware of the size of the paper, the layout of the words, and so the scales and depths. It reminds us of the fluidity of language, and encourages the use of setting a pen to paper to retain a sense of decorum when we express our feelings to another, whether this be for business or a personal affair.

Therefore, while a computer isolates people, a book can be seen to encourage their interaction when one person engages another to buy or borrow it and so extend skills of interaction. If they are polite and courteous, the transaction is a happy affair, which lifts their interaction with others. If the transaction has a rudeness or inconsideration, the book may well be cast at them, bringing with it an unpleasantness that disturbs the happiness of meeting other people. Both these good and bad experiences are vital to keep the individual tuned to the needs and considerations of others. Unfortunately, there is a growing awareness that our computer-raised children are becoming increasingly self-absorbed and narcissistic.[80] May we realise here that the deterioration of interactive skills is a very serious problem of our electronic age, because a community is held together by the sharing of mutual respect.

I witnessed how easily this poor communication in social skills can develop when I saw a group of school children sitting on a local train in a highly technological society. The children sat next to each other, and yet they sent text messages within their group instead of verbally talking. The novelty of texting had caught and taken them over, so that this now became their normal means of exchanging thoughts and feelings with a simple happy or sad icon being used by one child to another to express their feelings. It was a very satisfying experience to move from this society to one with less technology and witness children engaging each other through touch, talk, and laughter.

Electronic messaging, in any form, can be seen to be more detrimental than beneficial. While electronic messaging abbreviates and so limits the exchange of feelings and understandings, it also opens people up to unqualified abuse. Strangers text awful messages to people they do not know. It is one thing for a troubled child to go up to another and say to their face, " I don't like you." It is far more dangerous to society when that child can hide themselves and send cruel and despicable comments 30 times a day, day after day. The psychological disturbance deeply affects and conditions both of them.

With little feedback to control the ramifications it creates, this behaviour becomes acceptable to the mind of the sender and destructive to that of the recipient. However, it is not just a few nasty words that are transmitted, for these contain energy. This energy builds up a reservoir of sentiment that, like all energy, does not disappear and only transforms itself as it circulates. Limiting the use of computers in school retains physical interaction with information, and with this, a relatively higher social skill. Children do need guidance from an adult in this.

To believe that each child can sit in their class and learn their lessons through their own computer, with a teacher overseeing and guiding them when they have a problem, presents a false image of reality. Students will easily drift from the purpose of their lesson to explore unrelated information, as they have always tried to do. They will learn to copy information more than construct it themselves, and so forfeit the originality that gives them their personal identification in the design and use of this information.

We would be naive to think that a shifting presence of the teacher would not diminish their purpose; after all, the historical record of accountants in education has demonstrated how they consistently sought to reduce the cost of human labour. As computers take over the workload of teachers, their necessity will be less valued and their presence will diminish. The mind of the accountant would reason that if children learn through a computer, why not increase the students in a class to 100? If this, then why not let children learn from home, attending school once or twice a week for basic guidance and counselling?

Therefore, we should not look upon computers as simply developing keyboard skills, which are required ever more in our work today. While it is true that people learn skills from the tasks they accomplish, it is far truer that a person's perspective of the world around them and the skills they develop from that interaction become oriented through those tasks. We may more simply say that the way the individual orients themselves in an environment will determine how their intelligence and behavioural skills develop.

In realizing this, we should be wary that since computer information can only retain its attraction through increasing stimulation, it has the potential to drive human skills to change from actively engaging knowledge through the personality of others (with all the developed skills this entails), to passively waiting for the next mind influence that will cause the generation of a response.

- We like to think that we are using the computer program, though it needs to be asked if the program is actually using us. A computerized education, therefore, will condition the child to learn in "relative" isolation, by which they will learn to solve problems without reliance upon others and so develop lower skills of compassion and tolerance. These are the very values that hold a society together.

Since computer programs survive in a very competitive market by better stimulating the mind, with the more recent ones having to be more entertaining than the ones before it, just as movies had to be, the difference between a learning program and a video game is becoming less and less discernible. Because of this, and more importantly because I meet an increasing number of parents who have realized how the personality of their child has changed in an unhappy way through their playing of video games, it will be meaningful for us to understand what such electronic programs are doing to our children. I find it quite disturbing to realise how an innocent and charming child can become an uncontrollable demon, once the influences of a video game take them over.

The first thing we need to understand is that video games are not simply exciting. A study way back in 1998 showed that playing video games causes the release of the neurotransmitter dopamine in the brain. This is a pleasure-related chemical, and its release in this example has parallels to the effects gained from stimulant drugs such as amphetamine and methylphenidate.

However, while the rush of excitement the player feels is only temporary, it nevertheless means that through this stimulation, their brain is producing excessive amounts of dopamine. As the brain monitors what is happening, it seeks to counter this abnormal rise by lowering the normal production of this most critical neurotransmitter in its day-to-day activity.[81] In effect, this means that excessive playing of video games does alter the production of neurotransmitters in the child's brain, and that this may decrease their ability to process other types of information. In *"Brain Plasticity,"* we explain the role and functions of neurotransmitters and how they relate to the development of intelligence as their production levels rise or fall.

We may understand through this aspect of brain development why video games are so highly and in a sense dangerously addictive, after all, the child's brain patterns have been changed as they became somewhat dependent upon their interaction with them. It makes sense, in understanding this, why children can object strongly and even violently to a parent who tries to control their playing of video games if they have waited too long to take this control. Not all video games, of course, are of such concern, but many of them are. Take, for example, a recent study that found that some 80% of Nintendo and Sega Genesis games have aggression or violence as an objective of the game.[82] We may be led to wonder from this, if this addiction can have an even deeper meaning to a child's brain activity?

In 2011, Wang conducted a number of MRI studies (or magnetic resonance imaging) on the brains of children who were playing games for some 10 hours a day and was able to show clear images of brain disturbance. After just one week of monitoring children playing violent video games, he was able to show a decrease of activity in the frontal regions of the brain related to personality and cognitive processing.[83] This finding was supported by further MRI studies in China, which found that children who played 10 hours a day, compared to those who played only 2, had less developed regions in their brains that deal with such thinking processes.[84] In simpler words, we may understand from this that too much video game playing makes the child less able to process general information. To our interests, this means that when our children play video games too much, they are less likely to follow the progress of their lessons and so be more likely to fall behind in their academic progress. Over time, this can have very long-term consequences to their school grades and so to their opportunities in life. The problem, of course, is how to ease the child out of this addiction.

The first thing the parent should do, as Amy Paturel suggests, is to keep tabs on what their child is using the computer for, which they can do by learning how to check the computer's search history. According to a report from the Centre for Internet and Technology Addiction, the average child spends less than 20 percent of their computer time on academic-related activity.[85]

The next thing, and many parents will know only too well how difficult this can be, is to control the time their child spends playing computer/video games. It is important that the parent keeps control over this issue from the very beginning, because if they give in, in the early stages, it will become very difficult to regain that control once their child's brain has become subjected to the addiction process we have described.

Some psychologists suggest discussing with the child means of helping them to control their gaming activities, but as I have already pointed out, the objective of "the game" is to take over the personality of the player, and with the pull of the game and pressure from other children, an open discussion may not always render the best solution. I was once faced with this problem, and it came into my life so abruptly and so devastatingly that I felt I had to take very drastic action to solve the problem before it escalated.

When my children were about twelve years old, I thought about how they could learn through computer games. This seemed all very interesting, and so I bought them a game console, and selected a game where they could travel to different cultures to collect various items in order to complete the game. All this went very well, and we had great fun. We bought another game, and I thought this was all well and good too. However, I then bought them a rather expensive action game, left them to play it and went to my study upstairs to work. It seemed only a short time before I heard squabbling, shouts, and then the obvious sounds of fighting. I raced down, realized this fighting had started over the game they were playing, and disconnected the cables to prevent any more playing. The children calmed down very quickly, and started playing with normal activities. Peace and quiet came back to my home.

A week passed and I had thought they had learned their lesson. Unfortunately, I had not learned mine. I explained to them that we had to have more patience with each other, and to have fun with the game. I reconnected the cables, left them to play their game and went to my study. I think I had only just sat down with a cup of coffee, when it seemed that World War Three had erupted downstairs. I raced down to find my girls fighting tooth and nail with each other. I knew that I had to take this entire game thing out of our lives. I unplugged the game console, took it outside, and threw it away. I knew that I did not want this influence in our lives. My children would continue to play and make their own adventures as they had always done.

At first, I was worried about how my children might react, but to my utter and complete amazement, each had simply gone into their room and was found to be happily reading a book. I had not tried to discuss with them what to do, because I knew that they had been so under the control of this game device that they could not keep to any reasoning they might make. So, I took it out of their lives, and they grew up to be normally developed and happy children. I made time for them, which is a key issue here, and we shared fun and adventures.

Fortunately, my children had not developed into a game circle, where their social identity was reliant upon their gaming activity, but I know that if they had, I still would have done the same thing, and created other peer activities for them to develop through.

The solution I came up with may not be the ideal one for every family or for every child, but it worked for my children. Each parent must, of course, evaluate the life of their own child and the actions they should take to help their child through the dangers of video gaming. It is important for parents reading this to know that they are not alone. As I have mentioned, I meet many parents who work hard, love their children, and suddenly realise how playing computer games has taken over the life and purposes of the child they worry about.

One mother in Malaysia discussed this with me on Skype, and while her son was too far into the gaming matrix to be abruptly disconnected from it, as I had been able to do with my children, I was able to help him find a balance with game playing and his school work. As more parents are realizing how computer games are changing the personality of their children, and as they become more aware of how their school performance can be affected by such playing, more help is being made. Most societies now offer outpatient therapy or even intensive residential boarding schools to help children escape from a phenomenon that has more serious implications than we realise to the development of our children's intelligence and how their personality becomes constructed.

In returning to our discussion on computer programs in education, we are led from what we have just discussed, be aware that children profit differently from their interaction with them according to the level of reasoning developed within them.

Mason, for instance, found that students who reflect on the justification of knowledge more, as with undergraduates, do gain a higher understanding of the information they obtain through computers than students who accept information.[86] This was supported by Barzilai, who also found that the evaluatist thinker paid more attention to the authenticity and validity of online sources than the dualistic thinker.[87] This is to say that the student in general education accepts the information they gain from Internet sources in the same manner as they accept information from their teacher. In other words, a computer education does not evolve their ability to reason.

This takes us back to Perry's perspective on how education diversifies the thinking and reasoning ability of its students. We can see from this the possibility of how computers in school can actually increase the division between student ability, and how this would complement one of the original purposes of the general education as it grew out of the Industrial Revolution. The purpose was to prepare two categories of citizen based on their educational ability to reason. This brings us back to the consideration we have only just raised: What type of people will children become who are raised on television entertainment and computer games, and in school on software programs, where, in both environments, they see human skills as of secondary importance?

This is a question that asks us to reflect upon the ability of the adult in society to reason, when the child in the classroom will not be taught to develop through skills of peer reasoning, but individually, upon set programming levels. In turn, we are led to consider that the greatest danger with computers in education is not computers, but in the fading role and purpose of the teacher that they create.

Consider how the ability of the teacher to be so sensitive in how they share their thoughts and stimulate those of their students was being very much tested during the time of the pandemic.

After all, lesson planning for the teacher was not as straightforward as it was previously. They struggled to be far more inventive in how they presented their lesson and how they could get their students involved. Indeed, class discipline was harder to manage, with some students being deliberately unhelpful if not offensive. It was difficult for many teachers to keep the attention and interest of their students when they were in class, but online learning brought them many more challenges. Students were not always online on time, could interrupt the lesson due to a technical difficulty (a signal drops out), or could pretend there was one and then would need more time and help to understand what they missed. All of which confounded the smooth running of the lesson, demanding of the teacher further effort to help all their students keep up and so avoid being subjected to criticism for their failure to do so.

Although perhaps the biggest change from the pandemic came to the parents, particularly the mothers. Before the pandemic, a mother would drop her child off at 8 in the morning and pick them up at 3.30 in the afternoon. Providing the child was happy, the parent would have assumed they had had a good learning day, but with online teaching, the mother could monitor the teacher while her child was learning and involve herself. As she learned to be more sensitive in her awareness of how to help her child, she became more engaged in their learning and so could, for example, prompt them to ask questions, encouraging them to be more aware of how sensitive they were to what they were learning, or of what was happening at a moment. This awareness I regard to be a skill and so name it "The Art of Sensitivity in Awareness." We will examine this in detail in our following chapter and understand how this underlies the whole ability of the student to learn, just as it does the teacher to teach.

It is the student, however, who faced the greatest difficulty in the pandemic. Their whole conceptualization of learning was turned upside down. School was a place they went to learn, and home was their place where they could escape from learning, but then they had to reorient their mind to organize themselves to learn from home. Much depended on the support the child got from their parents in this, much of which decided how well they settled into their new home learning. If their room was quiet, ordered, and they were given a strict timeframe, they attended their lessons with a focused mind. On the other hand, they may have had to share the room with other siblings and be distracted by noises from different sources.

All this was at the surface level, for if we consider deeper levels of how the effectiveness of teaching and learning was impacted, then, we may see how the whole concept of sensitivity in awareness struggled to exist, with teachers finding it hard to pull all the minds of their students into the numerous steps of the lesson they had to work through. Online education sounded impressive, educationalists had to sell it this way, but it is not as effective for group learning as in-class, because the essential ability for the teacher to interact with each student is very much reduced.

The disturbing reality to all this was that too many educationalists, or at least policy makers, sold online teaching and learning as having benefits; after all, huge savings were made in running costs, and so saw education in the future to be one of a hybrid system, a mixture of in-class learning with online backup classes.

Personally, I could think of nothing more disastrous in the development of students struggling to learn without the immediate and personal attention of an ever-present teacher who understands the "Art of Sensitivity in Awareness" as we shall shortly discuss.

Today, we think of the purpose of the teacher as being only to give academic instruction, but the original purpose of the teacher was to instill in children moral guidelines by which they could better behave as responsible citizens in their society. This understanding has become lost to us, but we shall come to see, as our account unfolds, how education needs to reconsider the means by which it prepares the child for the role they will take as a citizen when their society is computer-controlled.

As our global world falls ever more under the operational influence of computers, as it must do, it is not the said intelligence of the individual citizen that will be of concern to the operational efficiency of their societies, because artificial intelligence will increasingly take this responsibility, but the need for the future citizen to be more self-responsible in how they think and to have a far greater awareness in how they reason in all the interactions they make.

This can only come through education, but only once educationalists themselves are caused to understand why their concepts of teaching and learning are rooted in a bygone age. If we are to be fair to the innocent child who now enters the institution we call learning, then we owe it to ourselves and to them to understand what this really means. As the pages of this book have helped us to understand the reality of education, let us now, and finally, come to understand how we may begin to bring change to it.

Chapter Thirteen
The Mind of the Student

As you will now understand, school does not work on the intelligence of students, where the cleverer ones receive top marks and the less intelligent ones receive the lowest marks. Earlier in this book, we used the term intelligence many times. As we will now see, the ability of the student in school is not decided by what is assumed to be their intelligence, but by how they are caused by their teachers to understand and to have the desire to learn and to keep up with the many, many rules of school, because it is these rules that give them the tools to think.

The school works on two specific languages. Mathematics and the language used for normal communication, be it English or German etc. These languages operate through rules.

To progress through their education, the student has to learn these rules, for they provide them with the tools in how to think and in how to present their thoughts.

In addition, they must learn facts of information. The more interested they are in the subject, the more sensitive they will be to how this information is defined, and by this will develop their own means of memory and so association by which they recognise purposes to this information.

As a child moves through the many years of their schooling, they are given more and more complex rules and facts to learn. As they struggle to understand the meaning of each new rule and so handle how to think with it, a new direction and control is imposed upon them in how to tackle information.

As each struggles to adapt to the way of thinking this brings, so they struggle to maintain their understanding of who they are, because whatever they do, it has their personality woven within it. Ever wary of the constant assessment made of their ability to show proficiency with this rule in the presence of the teacher and in a highly competitive environment, where others are ready to criticize them, the child's courage to be creative is tested.

Those who, by guidance and their own effort, master the use of these rules, develop a more acceptable identity in how they think. With the confidence of success, they strategically adapt their knowledge of these rules to creatively explore. With developed insight, they gain a sense of genius, which so very, very few attain.

The far greater mass never develops such proficiency with rules, and with the constant insecurity this brings, they lack the confidence to strategically explore. They become ever more a part of the unrecognizable grey mass, who show fewer and fewer sparks of enlightenment as the years pass.

It was because this was not understood that all means to improve student learning were developed through philosophies such as those of Piaget, Bloom, Gardner and Kolb with Learning Styles that were built upon the concept that ability is to some extent inherited and that learning is therefore a matter of teaching the student to orientate themselves to an environment as best as they are able. Gardener, of course, accentuated this reasoning with his theory of multiple intelligences.

However, as I have explained here and do so in great detail in "Intelligence: The Great Lie," our understanding of inherited intelligence is very wrong, as it evolved through political ideologies in the 19th century.

- Through my own and very vast experiences in learning, I take the stance that it is not how the student orientates themselves to the environment that is most important, but more of how they can become a living part of it in their mind. It is through the detail in awareness they desire to develop, are guided in how to do this, and, of great importance, how they are able to distance their mind from the distractions that play on them, which so limit their sensitivity to be aware of what is happening, that is what learning is about in education. Nothing more.

From this point of view, the student has to be acutely aware of very fine details. Such that it is through the sensitivity they develop in how they are aware of the learning task, be this how to understand the correct vowel to spell with or understand how to transpose a variable in Calculus, that is what actually determines their competence with it.

Thus, whether a student displays great competence in a subject or a very minimal level has nothing to do with the gene quality they may be imagined to have inherited. Instead of this, their competence came through the history of the strategies they have developed to interact with information, and the struggles of their mind to balance their confidence against their worries, which caused them to be finely aware of how to relate to information or to be distracted from doing so.

The ability of the student's brain to recognise and select the more relevant information and so make sense of it in order to respond to a question from their teacher or complete some assignment they will be evaluated on is not, then, decided by the quality of genes they may be thought to have inherited. It is most simply decided by the quality of the interest they have to enjoy this information, and so the purpose they personally have in doing so, as they have the confidence to develop their understanding through open dialogue.

There lies in this simple explanation all the reasons that cause different students to gain different quality of grades in school, and so all that follows from this in later life. Let us, therefore, return to understand more of how the mind drives the operations of the brain, by which the student understands and shares their understanding, as they are to be evaluated.

As we considered in the very beginning of this book, the ability of the student to focus upon that which they are required to learn and to know depends upon their mind's satisfaction of the two basic questions it continually seeks to ask itself.

- Am I safe?

and

- What is the most interesting thing for me at this moment?

In brief and in the first instance, the mind will be constantly seeking to know if the physical body or the social identity and so security of the individual is safe. Therefore, if the mind of a student is trying to find a way to settle a problem at home, resolve some personality issue with other students about them, as they most often are, or if they feel any insecurity from their teacher, it will not feel safe. In this state, their mind will be distracted from making a clear and precise interaction with what the student is trying to learn. In the simplest sense, this is to say they will be distracted from understanding a part of a lesson and possibly the whole meaning of it.

The second factor, where the mind seeks entertainment, is just as simple to understand. Yet, it is just as much little realized by the teacher if they broadcast their information, without consideration to the language skill and level of development of each individual student in their class, and so generally fail to make their lesson more interactively interesting than thoughts that can pull the minds of their students away from theirs.

Thus, in regard to the first instinct "Am I safe?" it is necessary now to understand that the mind is continually seeking to protect the survival of the body against physical or social dangers, such as injury to identity, loss of self-respect, etc. There are three areas of interest to us in this respect.

The home: If the child is experiencing any disturbance to their sense of security, such as any kind of abuse, be it verbal or physical, parents continually arguing, or parents separated, their mind can be seeking to understand how to resolve this to gain a sense of safety.

The Classroom: The classroom is a very competitive environment as students are continually vying for the teacher's attention. I see this right throughout education, from kindergarten to adult corporate learning. The belief that their marks may be influenced by a "better" acquaintance with the teacher, even though most teachers would deny this, is common in the mind of the student. Yet, I know from personal experience how a teacher can pull down the marks of a student they have some displeasure with - such is the reality of human nature. However, this necessary striving for higher grades does prompt some students to seek to discredit others, as they seek to make themselves appear more favourable to the teacher or even to their peers.

It is easy to understand from this how all manner of seeking to discredit a student can be easily engineered through social rejection to physical bullying, which the teacher needs to be acutely aware of. We must expect it. We must search the eyes and hearts of our students, ever suspecting them. Find it. Deal with it, and you have the attention of the concerned student for your lesson and also their respect for you for many years later.

The Teacher: Teachers are human beings. They can be loving, kind, selfish or vindictive. I have experienced all types. Broadly speaking and apart from their nature, there are two kinds of teachers. There is the teacher who knows how to engage the minds of their students in a stimulating manner, and there is the kind of teacher who feels they have to use authority to gain the compliance of their students to learn. The latter teacher, of whom there are very many, and certainly if their nature is not loving and sincere, does not understand and probably does not know what we explain in this chapter.

If the student "feels," and we must place great emphasis upon what the individual feels, that they are "not safe" in one or more of the above areas, then their mind will be thinking about how to bring a level of harmony about to gain the sense of safety it needs. By this distraction, they will fail to bring their senses to focus highly upon the audio or visual information expected of them to learn. Thus, they will hear but listen or look and not see, to some greater or lesser extent. This is the factor of sensitivity we have just mentioned.

Imagine now a student who has long felt security in all of the above areas, or has somehow managed to compensate for a failing in one by drives promoted in others, and was so inspired by their teacher or driven by some inner need to focus precisely on information.

As their audio or visual senses become tuned to monitor information, they have learned through feedback how to precisely identify the most relevant. This selected information is then relayed to their memory banks, where it is associated very precisely with information that was previously stored with great precision. Thus, each parcel of incoming information is accurately related to previously stored information, and by this high level of association, it can be quickly evaluated for all purposes it may have. This is an ongoing process for the student, and they will be recognised to be the best in the class, unless some sense of insecurity arises in one of these areas they are not able to compensate for.

Providing this does not happen, they will respond quickly and accurately to a question asked, and providing they are given the confidence in the learning atmosphere, which can be very hard to obtain in a class, they will seek to better understand their response by inquiry. Through their drives, they will have developed very good strategies to interrogate information and so will have developed very good memory systems, which, by their continual interest, will keep this stored information alive and easily accessible. This student we would call intelligent.

However, to "think" that one student is intelligent is to suggest that others they are being compared to are less so. This is where we fall into the trap of thinking that a quality of intelligence is related to learning in school. It is not. Let us, then, consider the other students this one is being compared to.

Each of these other students will have struggled to find harmony in one of the three areas in earlier lessons, maybe within the past year or quite possibly right throughout their school life. They may, for example, have started school with poor language skills or have been poorly prepared for school with a low level of mental discipline that caused them to fall behind on day one.

Go into a kindergarten class and it is strikingly obvious to see some infants calm and focusing their attention on the teacher, while others are running around living within their own interests and desires. In fact, all of school life may be thought to be like this, the only difference being that older children, albeit students, have learned they are not free to physically move from their chairs. Yet, their minds still drift to thoughts other than those the teacher is expecting of them, all because either or both of the two instincts of the mind have not been met.

Thus, all students, less than that one or those few who had learned to play the game, lack control over the distresses or distractions in their life and failed for one of a multitude of reasons to give their earnest attention to minutely examine the information they had been given.

As they heard what the teacher told the class but did not listen, or scanned text instead of examining the relationships of letters and words to clearly define meanings, they vaguely selected information. This vaguely defined information was then relayed to their memory banks, where it tried to find relationships with information previously stored that was also vaguely selected and associated. When such a student is asked a question, they struggle more to see relationships and meaning to the information at hand, but because they will be aware of rejection from others in the class or an impatient teacher, so they will lack the confidence to better understand what is asked of them.

Too often, such a student will reply with a "I don't know," instead of replying, "Could you please ask me in a different way?" In such a way, it would most likely help them to better define information and seek an appropriate response. There again, such a student would most likely not have had their confidence raised to so inquire in the class.

Competence in a particular subject can be related to the environment of the class, which is usually the teacher, while competence within the school year will be dependent upon the student being able to overcome the distractions they face in the three areas just outlined. Incidentally, it was, as we mentioned earlier, Spearman's complete misunderstanding of this that gave him the idea to invent the g and s factor of intelligence, which set much of the foundations for the concept of IQ testing.

Spearman believed, as a disciple of Galton, both of whom we discuss in our book *"Intelligence,"* that we inherit a factor of intelligence. In witnessing that students tended to gain similar scores in many subjects, Spearman reasoned this was evidence of what he called the general or g factor of intelligence. It is not. It is simply evidence of the levels of competence developed through the tender balance each human being could make between the distractions they face and the drives they have to succeed.

However, the failure of the student to concentrate with accuracy on information is actually far more sophisticated than simply thinking they are not concentrating. To understand this, we need to discuss a little of neural chemistry and so gain a little insight into the relationship between the mind and the brain, and so how learning can be very, very easily inhibited.

Before all in this chapter can gain relevance in how the student really learns, and so how the **'rules'** of school work, which give them the 'tools' to know how to think in school and successfully navigate through their learning, we first need to discuss one of the most important aspects of learning that is generally not known -- if at all it is.

Chapter Fourteen
The Effect of Bullying or Social Humiliation

I think this is the most important chapter in the whole book. When we are happy and calm, our body works in the parasympathetic mode. We analyze information according to our interests and the distractions we can control. In this condition, we have no problem learning, provided it is presented in a stimulating manner.

However, when we sense danger, we move into the sympathetic mode. In this condition, our mind tells our brain to send out signals to release certain hormones. A social threat to our identity triggers the release of a hormone called cortisol. The purpose of cortisol is to make us think about a danger to keep ourselves safe. We know it is there, and we can choose how to respond to it through our experiences. A physical threat to our physical well-being could generate many hormones, including adrenaline, which would give us a surge of energy to fight or flee.

When cortisol is released into the brain, it moves into areas that we use for reflective thinking, such as "Should I write the sentence this way or that way?" "What is the best word to use here?" and so "If I move this variable there, would that give me the correct answer in the math problem?"

Once here, it blocks these parts of the brain from operating clearly, depending on the level of threat to the individual. If the threat is slight, perhaps someone talking about them, cortisol will allow them to partly think about what they are learning, and partly about the cause of the stress.

However, if their perception of the social danger is very high, a bully threatening them or a teacher humiliating them in front of the class, cortisol can completely flood these areas to prevent any kind of casual thinking and totally open up other areas of the brain, forcing them to think only of the cause of the stress. If this happens, they will not be able to think about anything to learn. Their mind will be a complete blank. They would literally feel their brain is frozen.

Their brain literally freezes.
They cannot think about what they are trying to learn.

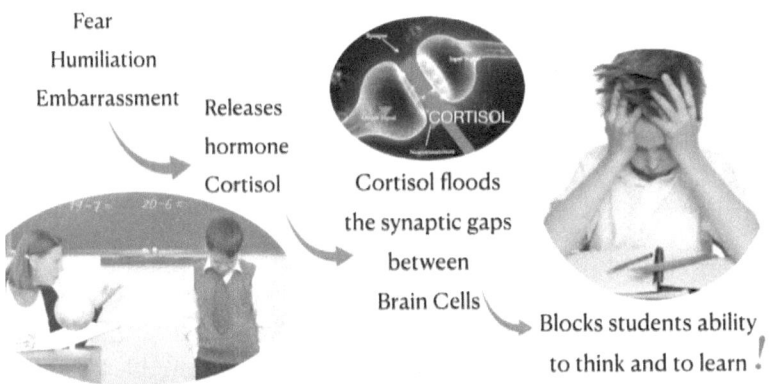

- It is extremely important in the highest sense that all teachers know of this phenomenon and are continually alert to it happening in any of their students.

- The cause of cortisol rising is a real danger to a student failing to clearly understand what they should be thinking about. This can all too easily prevent them from keeping up with their learning. It is NO small thing, for as it disturbs their learning, so it affects their class marks. If their thinking is continually disturbed by bullies in the class, their examination grades will be lower than they could otherwise be. This, of course, will affect their later opportunities in life.

The mind, however, does not simply switch off the sympathetic mode once the danger has passed. If the mind considers the danger may come again, it will be constantly preparing the nervous system to be ready for immediate action. Therefore, in the case of a student being bullied, being continually threatened, abused, embarrassed, or ridiculed, this prevalent danger causes their mind to constantly keep the nervous system in a constant state of readiness for their self-protection.

It is easy to see from this why the mind of a student who is bullied is constantly living in a state of stress. After all, they expect the bully to cause them physical pain or social embarrassment the next time they meet them. This constant worry, working throughout the day, during the night, and in their dreams, changes the threshold level of the chemicals in their brain.

To different individuals, having had different experiences, this means different things, but in general, it means that the mind of the victim is in a constant state of alert to behavioral danger and therefore cannot think clearly in their learning. The same principle applies to children who suffer domestic concerns, the most common of which could be a parent shouting at them, or far worse, suffering abuse.

The effect of this constant or recurring worry on the learning development of the student is too little recognised, and yet it can bring disaster to their ability to learn.

Let us say a student is happy and can give a high level of attention to a math problem. They are constructive in their thoughts as to how they should move numbers about. However, if they should feel disturbed by another, let's consider a situation where another student says something hurtful about them, or just as much, a teacher humiliates them in front of the class. Even something as slight as this can cause their brain to change how it gives attention to their mind.

Once injury or embarrassment enters their thoughts, the student's ability to concentrate on the math question they are working on suddenly drops. Now, their thinking is divided between those who are injuring them and what they are trying to learn. This change of attention can be very short or it could be very, very long, lasting perhaps the whole lesson -- if not the whole day. If they are exposed to even slight but regular attacks, this state could persist within them for many years.

I remember a young lady who joined an adult class. She was happy and wanted to learn. She was constantly engaging with others and helping them. Three men thought it fun to make small remarks about her. As soon as she heard these, she burst into tears and ran out of the class, extremely distressed. Once I had helped her calm down, she explained how she had been sexually assaulted by her stepfather for many years. These men did not know it, but their behaviour triggered off the fear that the lady tried to hide from herself to live a normal, happy life.

As long as they suffer psychological attacks, their ability to learn will suffer.

If, in the following lesson, the victim fears being injured again, they will be thinking of the source of this harm and less about what they should be learning. If those who hurt them leave them alone and they can regain a sense of security, they may be able to get back into their learning and hopefully keep up, but it is not always the case.

However, if those who hurt them continue to do so, they will continually struggle with their focus on the bully. This seriously affects their ability to learn. I know of very many experiences relating to this. Yet, it is not only another student who can trigger the rise of cortisol.

Too often, a teacher may lose their temper with a student and embarrass them. I have heard of many instances where a teacher shouts at a student in class, calling them "stupid," and I have witnessed this a few times myself. When this happens, cortisol levels rise in the student's brain, and they can lose confidence in their ability to learn. They may start to hate attending that teacher's classes. It might be surprising how often this occurs. The human mind is very fragile.

Therefore, when such a student is troubled in their lessons, they cannot be calm enough to be sensitive to things that interest them, or to a teacher trying to explain the meaning of some point. They can grasp at things, but their mind is too erratic to follow detail. It is constantly searching for and analyzing a possible danger.

With this stress upon them, it means the student struggles to see the connection between things in their lessons, and just as much later when doing their homework. Too easily, do they gain a poor understanding from their learning experience. As one lesson builds upon another, their ability to learn is restricted by what they misunderstood previously. As time passes, their marks go down and their grades fall.

Therefore, as a teacher, try to get your students to feel safe and happy in your lessons. Find ways to make them laugh, because when they laugh, cortisol returns to a normal level, and they can concentrate on their learning.

Chapter Fifteen
The Rules of Learning

When we think of school, we think of students learning. When a student does not perform as well as we hoped, we look for evidence in how well they learned. How was their behavior and attitude? How well did they complete assignments? When we think in these terms, we too easily fall into the trap of believing that each student succeeds more or less in accord with the quality of intelligence they inherited.

When a student does well, it is normal to see their parents doing well in life. Their social success seems natural, perhaps something they were born with, but also helped by the money they have. When a student does not do well in their studies, and we see their parents with obvious money problems, and perhaps not well-behaved, we wonder how we can help the student. We try ways, but these don't seem to make much of a difference. Then, from the back of our mind, the thought rises, *Perhaps, they were born like this?* After all, this would explain why they don't easily understand when others instantly do. Once this thought arises, we conclude that we cannot undo what nature has done. We did our best, but are too aware of the 30 or 40 other students demanding our time, and the lesson will soon end. We move on. Time has run out.

We used to talk openly like this, but times have changed. Now, we are more conscious of offending someone and of political inferences, by which we could be sued. So, instead, we think of some other reason to explain why a student did or does not do so well. More often than not, this is in some domestic or social-environmental problem. Yet, when we think like this, we are only doing so at the surface level.

If we truly want to help our students and enable each one to succeed far better in education, then we need to understand how schools really work. To do this, we need to delve deeper into the operational mechanics of the school to understand how it manages to process students to create the illusion we witness. Because how the school works really is an illusion created for us to believe that it is teaching all students to learn, while really secretly categorizing them into future work potential. After all, this is why society funds education, not primarily for the betterment of the child.

Therefore, instead of thinking that school educates students in certain subjects, understand that all these subjects are based on and revolve through two languages. These are the language of mathematics and the language used for communication in the school. This may be English, Chinese, Arabic, etc. Competence in these languages depends upon the understanding and practice of each of the numerous rules that each language is based upon. We mentioned this earlier, but here we come to really understand this.

Take, for example, Mathematics. In the language of Mathematics, this is to know the rules to correctly transpose numbers. If the student learns these rules, they will have the "tools" to successfully work through a learning exercise. They will know how to think! Solving one problem after another, they gain confidence. They discover they are good at this; therefore, they enjoy doing it. From here, they will be inspired to want to explore and develop their knowledge. With the confidence they now believe in themselves, they become creative in making applications of this rule into areas of other subjects. Being good in mathematics ensures they will be good in the applied sciences that require knowledge in how to work with formulas and equations, etc. So, they become good in physics and chemistry too.

Let us look at two students of equal intelligence to see why one appears to be more intelligent than the other, when they are not

Consider the following equation:

$$6/2(2+1) =$$

The student Gini was listening to the teacher when he explained to the class the rule of BODMAS. This rule requires the student to do the brackets first, then work from left to right as they follow the order to divide, multiply, add, or subtract numbers. She listened and practiced this rule to become proficient with it.

So, in finding the answer to this question, Gini did the brackets (2+1) to obtain 3. She then followed the order by dividing 6 by 2 to get 3. Then, she multiplied 3 by 3 to give the answer of 9.

9 is the correct answer.

However, the student Mark was thinking about other things when the teacher was explaining this rule, and so was not really listening. There again, he may have been sitting on a row too far back from the teacher and could not feel the emotional connection to clearly relate his mind to what the teacher was trying to explain from their mind. For whatever reason, Mark MISSED the rule.

It is vital to understand he missed the rule!

So, when the other students in the class began to work through this equation, Mark used logic. First, he did the brackets (because he heard this part of the rule) and so got 3 by adding 2 to 1. But, the order to work from the left he did not hear, and so used common sense to multiply this 3 by 2 to get 6. Then, he divided 6 by 6 to get 1. Now, the answer One is completely wrong.

Mark failed this operation not because of his lack of intelligence, but because he did not follow the rules correctly.

The important point to realise here is that as he builds one misunderstanding or error upon another, his overall performance will be less than others in the class. In turn, he will believe less in himself and so fail to observe information precisely. He will develop less proficient memory networks and so struggle to remember facts.

In other words, his ranking in the class will not be very high, and since he could not respond with the right response and level of confidence to a question asked by the teacher, Mark will be thought to have less intelligence than Gini and other students who always seem to give the right answer.

All we say here for the rules of the language of Mathematics is exactly so for the rules of the language used in the educational system, whether this be English or whatever it may be.

Consider that **were** is the past tense of **are**, while **where** is related to the destination **there**, as in over there. Equally, a season is a common noun and not a proper noun, so a season begins with a lower-case letter. If a student does not learn these associated rules, they will write:

"Were where we last Summer?"
Instead of "Where were we last summer?"

By not knowing these rules, they will lose two marks in the mind of the teacher, and so gain lower grades than a student who has learned both these rules.

Accordingly, the effort the student puts into learning the rules of how to spell a word, the rules to know how to construct a sentence correctly (grammar and syntax), and how well they know the rules to tell a story when they present their mind, either verbally or in writing, will so determine the marks or grades they will be given.

Such evaluation of the student is also determined by facts they have remembered and know how to set these into their story.

As we saw with Lara, remembering facts is much related to the sensitivity she gave to the buildup of information. In turn, this was related to the interest she had while learning this information, and so the purpose or use she found for it.

Yet, her confidence to present her mind, and so to have the desire for this information, will lie in the competence she had developed with the rules of the language.

When students have been well taught the rules of the 3 R's and all that follows from these, so they will earn marks that encourage their interaction in learning. However, when these basics are not well taught, and sadly this is too often the case today, students often do not understand why they get too many red marked corrections. As they see these marks as a sense of failure, they lose interest in applying their effort to learn the subject. This happens when they do not understand that success in a subject is seated in their competence with the basic rules upon which information is laid.

So, while we may think that it is intelligence (to some unknown extent) that decides the marks and grades a student is awarded, it is in fact only the competence they have gained in the rules of the languages school works upon.

In fact, grades are basically earned by the quality of language a student has, plus their inner drive to want to learn to remember facts. Parents can make a great difference here if they know how to develop these two factors.

May we begin to ever more understand, from the little we have so far discussed, why intelligence is not simply "a thing" the child is born with, and thereafter develops by their genetic limitation. This will become ever clearer as we proceed through this book.

Therefore, evaluation in the academic world is only about how well the individual knows the rules of how to present information, and how they have learned to develop good memory structures through their interest. None of this has anything to do with whatever value of intelligence they may be thought to have inherited.

Indeed, solving problems is simply a matter of a long chain of experiences with different applications that brought insight. All of which, all of this, relies upon the individual developing competence with the rules of academia. Consider, now, how learning the rules of a language, and practicing them to become proficient, much decides the ability of the student and not so their assumed intelligence.

When the student learns and practices the rules, they:

- Can negotiate through a learning task.
- Interested to explore by themselves.
- Will ask more questions.
- Will interact more and share thoughts more.
- Develop high confidence.
- Be interested in remembering knowledge.
- They will develop better neural efficiency.
- Feel Inspirational. Be more creative and will carry the skills from this subject into other areas, and develop high academic performance.
- Get Good Marks/Grades.

However, when the student does not learn and and does not practice the rules, they:

- Feel lost in negotiating through a learning task.
- Be dependent on others, guiding them.
- Develop low Confidence.
- Will be reluctant to ask questions.
- Will be passive.
- Be little interested and develop poor memory.
- They will be casual in how they identify with information.
- Have no interest in the subject.
- Think the subject is boring and have little interest.
- Get Poor Marks/Grades.

It is a very valid point to mention here that developed countries spend huge amounts of money on making classrooms creative, in the belief that this will help students to learn better. Walls are decorated, creative desks and chairs are purchased to stimulate the students' minds, and they are provided with a vast array of creative implements to make learning fun and enjoyable.

Yet, nothing happens. We still find exactly the same range of ability in a class, where one or two will excel in their learning, most will struggle in their understanding, and one or two will struggle very hard to keep up or won't struggle at all. What is not understood here is that the environment does not make the student think creatively in their lessons, and it does not improve their ability to learn. This is only a philosophical idea proposed by psychologists and educationalists who do not understand how the school actually works. It works on rules.

Let's look at an example of two students, Mary who has learned the rules and Peter who didn't listen as they were explained to him, when they are told to write an essay on some topic.

Peter looks at the question. He starts to write from his heart. After a few lines, he gets stuck. He waits for an idea and adds this to what he has written.

Peter races to finish, believing he can impress his teacher and so earn a good mark. He does not. Let's see how Mary handles the task.

Mary looks at the question and asks herself what the question really wants her to do. She thinks about the best answer and the best ending. She has developed skills for instrumental rationality, which is defining the best goal. Mary, then, scribbles down thoughts for sub-goals. Once she has a schema in her mind, she writes a paragraph. Then another, ensuring its meaning flows clearly from one to the other.

Mary writes three more paragraphs and again goes over the flow of the text. She is constantly evaluating her presentation, being as creative as she can. When she comes to the end, she thinks of something that has meaning. She wants the teacher to be struck by her ending, because she knows this is what will much decide the mark she gets. Then, she does something Peter never thought of. Mary goes over everything, checking and checking, looking for the smallest mistake in spelling, word order, and punctuation. Then, she goes over everything again before she hands her paper to the teacher.

Peter never understands why he only ever gets a mark of 5/10, while Mary always gets 10/10. He just thinks she was born smart. You will now know the real reason. It is all about rules and rules and rules, learning, practicing and using them.

As we can see from the above, genuine creativity comes from inside the student when they know they are good at doing something and it is slightly challenging. This awareness is directly related to how well they listened to the explanation of a rule, practiced it to become proficient with it, and then kept it alive in their mind by occasionally using it, and so developing applications with it. This is the mind being creative.

Accordingly, lack of creativity and so misunderstandings, errors and lower performance come when the student is distracted in learning due to some problem at home, suffers some form of bullying, intimidation, or rejection in the class, or finds the teacher's lesson boring and can't keep their attention, as some 98 percent of students do.

In 1968, Land and Jaman conducted a study on the creativity and intelligence of 1,600 three-to-five-year-olds and found 98% displayed genius quality. They retested these children five years after they had begun school and found that now only 30% displayed a genius quality in their responses to questions asked. When the same children were tested after 10 years of schooling, only 12% now displayed genius creativity. In the testing of adults, in their early 30s, only 2% displayed the same quality of genius intelligence that 3-year-olds had.[88] How could this happen?

A simple explanation for this lies in the student's success with the rules by which the school operates, as we have just seen. When a student learns these rules and becomes proficient with them in a learning task, they feel a sense of achievement, which encourages them to want to explore. This is to be creative. However, as they fail to understand a rule, as most do, in the way it is taught or are distracted from focusing upon it, and so do not keep up with progressions of this rule, they do not have the tools to navigate through a learning task correctly. In being confused in what to do, they make guesses and create errors..

As the teacher marks these errors and grades them in the class, they feel insecure and fearful of embarrassment in the presence of their peers, they refrain from exploration. It is this curtailing of their confidence to explore that reduces their creativity. They are worried, nervous, even frightened of what to do next when others about them are likely to be critical.

So we may see that school actually reduces student creativity when all students do not keep up or are caused not to keep up with the rules that enable them to be successful in their academic studies. If, for a moment, we reflect on the real purpose of school to produce two levels of citizen worker, it could be seen that such reduction of creativity in the general mass of students supports the ideology behind this philosophy, for it sees that the society works better when creativity is left in the hands of the leaders, which is to say those who went to university and were schooled in higher reason.

Iserbyt brings this out in her book "The Deliberate Dumbing Down of America,"as she explains how education in America is designed to reduce student ability for political purposes.[89]

However, the importance of understanding the value of rules in a student's learning cannot be overemphasised, which is why students should never miss one lesson. Their competence with rules does explain why they vary in their performance in a class. Thus, a student's performance is not decided by their natural ability, but by the quality of the support they receive from their parents and their teachers. Everything, comes down to sensitivity in awareness!

For the parents, this is how well they prepared their child for school by the storytelling they developed within them, so their child learned how to explain their mind with great sensitivity and imagination. Also with the sense of orientation they raised them through, so they could easily adapt to a new environment and have the confidence to readily settle within it, and, then, by the mental stamina they developed within them so their child could stay focused and resist distractions as the rules of the languages began to build up. Once their child entered the school system and so moves through it, the parents are fundamental in helping them to keep balance with their learning and the activities they engage that will stimulate their awareness of the greater world that fuels their imagination.

By their teachers, it is the manner they have developed to present information in the social/domestic thinking language of each child. When they teach a class of 30 plus students, it is by the skill they have developed to share this information so that each student, regardless of their development of the subject, is able to understand and relate to this, and by the fun and stimulation they engage the minds of the class in so they will resist distractions and want to engage with great sensitivity in their learning.

It is, then, that the more we move away from the idea that intelligence has anything to do with a student's performance and move further into how their mind is prompted to engage their learning, that we come to far better understand what determines their competence and so the marks and grades they will gain, which will much determine the later role they will play in society. After all, the top students are only so because they have taught themselves. The rest lacked the self-confidence and drive to do so, and as one misunderstanding or error built upon another, so their ability merged into the grey average.

We mentioned the bell curve graph earlier, although this name comes from its shape. Its official name is the Standard Distribution Curve. In "Intelligence: The Great Lie", we go into great depth to understand the origins of this graph and how it was really developed to understand the positioning of stars in the sky.

However, if we apply this graph in education to explain the variation of grades or thought ability in any class, we could see it shown as so:

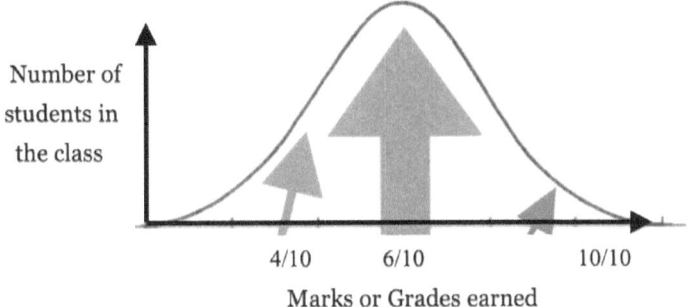

Marks or Grades earned

In fact, rather than now showing a range of ability or intelligence, all this graph really shows is a range of confusion.

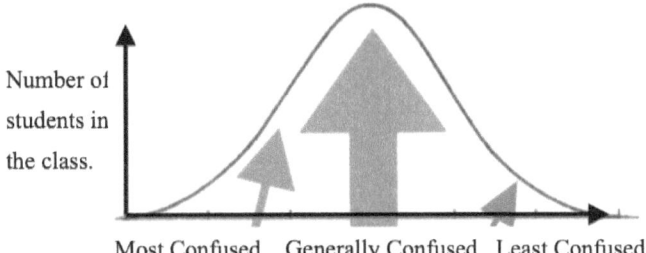

Most Confused   Generally Confused   Least Confused

The students represented by the dark blue are the cleverest. These are the ones thought to be the brightest or the smartest in the class. They are the least confused, because of a number of factors they kept up with the rules of the languages, developed very good memory structures through their interest, and developed very good skills in recognizing the application of information.

Often driven by an ego to want to succeed, they developed very precise networks of stored information. When asked a question, they had the self-confidence to argue a presentation and learned from any mistakes they made. These students effectively taught themselves. The best student is doing all they can to stay the best, while others will try to be like them or believe that they never can be.

The students represented by the lighter or grey blue did not keep up with all the rules as they developed. Because of a number of factors in their lives or in the class environment, they were distracted and did not have the confidence or drive to question what they did not understand. Their ability to know how to control information is much less than that of the high scorers.

The students to the left, represented by red, are the most confused. This is either because they came to school with poor language skills and found it difficult to relate to the languages of school as the rules built up, or because their minds are troubled and so distracted from concentrating in class by factors created inside or outside of the school. Remember: "Am I safe?"

These students seldom were or created a belief that they could be by role playing the situation they are in.

I hope that it is now very clear why competence in learning has nothing to do with intelligence and everything to do with the quality by which the mind of the student is caused to relate to the moving world about them. The key to understanding how we can help them better lies in what I term "a sensitivity in awareness," as it explains the real causes of the differences in student competence and, too often, any differences we seek to register in individual intelligence.

Chapter Sixteen
The Art of Sensitivity in Awareness

Let us see how these work for:
- The Teacher
- The Parent
- The Child or Student of any age.

The Teacher:

In the simplest terms, sensitivity in awareness can be seen as a method for the teacher to be in harmony with the student they are seeking to help, or with the class as a whole they are teaching. It is a way for the teacher to be sensitive enough to understand the life experiences of a student, to see the world of information as they do, and then to raise their perception through the greater experiences they have by making use of security, confidence. Once this trust has been gained, they can begin to reconstruct or better develop the student's understanding. With experience, the teacher is able to use this method beyond the individual student to orchestrate the understandings of the class as a whole.

When we realise that intelligence is not determined by inheritance in the ways we have come to understand and that school performance is a purely environmental ability, then, the true role of "sensitivity in awareness" becomes apparent.

By simple example, Bloom saw a number of stages that a student should move through to develop their competence in learning. First something must be remembered, then understood. Then, it is to be applied to other experiences through analyzing, evaluating and finally application to make creative understanding of it. Thus, two students will move through each of these stages and produce two different levels of competence, which will be largely said to be caused by their different intelligences.

However, this is where our most fundamental error lies, because these differences we witness are not caused by differences in intelligence, but most simply by the degree of interest and effort that each student applied in minute detail to each of the stages they moved through. For whereas one student was casual and little focused on what they were doing, the other took greater care in the examination of information and so recognised higher levels of meaning with it. As always, the determining factor is not what is done, but how well it is done according to the smallest detail.

In the simplest and most basic sense, awareness of "sensitivity in awareness" would significantly improve the abilities of the parent, teacher and student.

The teacher, for example, would be more aware of how to create a non-threatening learning environment, so their students do not feel intimidated, embarrassed, afraid, or uncomfortable. While the need for this may well be understood, the actual reason for it is less so, as we explained through the activity of cortisol. Therefore, a teacher who is able to be sensitive in their awareness of this can generate a learning environment where this disturbing brain activity does not occur, enabling all of their students to learn better.

In understanding this, the teacher would then be more aware of how to boost the self-esteem of each student, to inspire each to have the confidence to manage the learning tasks they will give them. This may seem an obvious need, but I have found this practice to be generally absent in the very many classes I have observed over the years. Teachers were simply not sensitive enough to the concerns of their students as each struggled to learn in a very competitive environment and struggled against the egos of others.

Finally, teachers are under a lot of pressure to complete the syllabus in time, but few seem sensitive to the trouble their students have in keeping up with this constant build-up of information. A teacher sensitive to this would incorporate strategies to keep the information from previous and past lessons ever prevalent, as they proceed through the year. If they were to do this, each student would have more chance to understand aspects they did not earlier, or correct misunderstandings; as all information is caused to be kept alive and relevant as the year proceeds. Should the teacher be sensitive to these three factors, then all of their students would be able to more keep up and understand their lessons better. In short, the overall learning ability of the class would improve.

The Parent:

"Sensitivity in awareness" has a slightly different perspective for the parent. A parent who is very sensitive to the development of their child will focus on creating security for them through love, develop very high language skills within their child and nurture their child to find reason for all they do.

The desire for the child to believe in themselves and in what they attempt to do is seeded in the security and love they obtain at home. This is continually tested in the learning environment, as they witness students appearing to deal with a learning task better than they believe they can. By the parent developing greater security within their child's mind, they give them a sense of who they are. This develops a greater ability for them to understand themselves in any new physical or social environment they are placed in and so how they may better adapt to survive. Within the classroom, this means they can better control distractions in order to place greater sensitivity into what they are learning, and so overcome failures without getting depressed and strive to be more successful in the future.

Having a greater vocabulary and ease in using it through the development of early literacy skills (reading stories and holding discussions with them to create awareness and narrative skills), inspires the child's imagination and confidence to express themselves in different ways in the same situation. This flexibility enables them to better control the situation to their advantage. They become better at word play in how to influence the thinking of others, which develops their confidence to interact with each learning task. This develops within them a greater sensitivity in dealing with different types of information. They become more competent.

When the parent explains to their child why they are attempting to do something, it helps their child to recognise a clearer purpose for this and define a better goal to achieve it. This educates the child to see a greater relationship with abstract information. As they do this, they develop to see how an unrelated concept can be brought into the concept they are trying to develop to make it more successful. This teaches them to better identify with sub-goals or the better steps to work through to achieve their aim. This is an essential thinking process that is little taught in school and yet it is the main component of their thinking process by which they will be evaluated and so graded by their teacher.

It is through the qualities of "sensitivity in awareness" that parents and teachers nurture their youth, which largely determines how successful each will be to learn in school.

The Student:

The student who has been caused to develop good levels of "sensitivity in awareness" will have their own purpose to learn what is expected of them. They will also have developed a very high precision in dealing with information and they will effectively have learned how to teach themselves.

At all ages, children attend school because they have to. They learn what they are told to learn, but little consideration is given from the parent or the teacher to be sensitive in how to motivate this learning through some higher purpose. If this is done sensitively, the student applies more effort because they are doing so for their purpose and not simply to appease the teacher.

A student may only identify with something they are trying to learn, through the accuracy by which they have recorded previous events similar to this. Thus, if they have developed to be sensitive in identifying with information, whether this be audio or visual, they will more precisely relay this higher definition to their memory. If they were equally sensitive in the processing of earlier information, then their memory banks will be clearly defined. This will enable new information to be readily related to stored experiences by which they will be able to quickly and accurately suggest a purpose to the new information they engage. In other words, they will appear smarter or more intelligent, but only so because they developed a very high level of "sensitivity in awareness."

However, a student who is vague in their selection of information (and the very most in every class are due to some form of distraction, lack of interest, or boredom), will process this to previously stored information in their memory that was equally vague. Due to the low sensitivity with which earlier information was selected and stored, they will have difficulty pulling in relationships with the new information to easily recognise an error or a precise purpose to it. In other words, they display less competence in dealing with a task and are graded less because of this.

Critical thinking is the "in thing" in education at the moment, and yet education of it very little alters the mental ability of students to so *think critically*, because such applications of it do not alter or so improve the general ability of the student in how they think.

It may be thought to be taught in a lesson, for example, by asking of the possible effects of two or more scenarios developing. Yet, this thinking is not transferred by the student into other topics and not into real life situations and therefore fails to fulfil its objective, which is to improve their skill in reasoning.

When it does not, so the difference in any two students is said to come down to the quality of intelligence they developed or more significantly inherited. If we want to so improve the reasoning skills of a student, which is essential if we want to improve their ability to relate to information, then, we need to help them to restructure the ways the neurons of their brain have developed networks of understanding. This is very simple to achieve, but only once we understand the importance of "sensitivity in awareness."

By being sensitive to a situation, the student as a human being will interact with it at a far higher level. As they recognise a higher level of achievement, they will develop more confidence to be more aware of what they did and the better result they obtained. It is this self-realisation of being more aware that causes them to be more critical in their evaluation in all aspects of life. Therefore, if we could invest more patience, compassion, and understanding into each student, they would most assuredly rise beyond the expectations previously held of them.

Let me share insight into how to actually develop the ability of your students, with nothing more than learning to be aware of sensitivity in awareness. Let me give examples to this:

σ a α.

So, we find a teacher teaching her students how to write the letter "a." This, of course, is only an example and could otherwise be a stage in calculus or a written composition. We focus here only on the minds of the student working with the mind of their teacher.

We see the little girl happy. She adores her teacher and wants to be like her. She writes her "a" the best way she can, and as near to the example given her. Now, the boy is happy too, but he wants to go and play football in the break. So, his mind is thinking about how to write the "a," but he is also thinking about his friends, the bell to ring, and who is looking after the ball. In other words, his mind is drifting. He is not concentrating on what he is doing, and by their degree of concentration, we can see how the girl's "a" is closer to the model given to them by the teacher than that of the boy's.

At the end of the lesson, the bell will ring, and the teacher will regard each student as having written the letter to the best of their ability, and so will notice a variation in understanding and effort. The teacher has done her job, and in the following lesson, she will move to the next stage in the learning process — how to write a "b" or whatever this happens to be.

As we can see, the boy's effort was disturbed by other factors on his mind, and so his degree of sensitivity in what he was doing was much less than that of the girl's. The problem for the boy is that in the next lesson and so the next year, this "a" will be taken as "his ability."

This is what he is thought to be capable of, and so the crux of the problem with every student. Such that the effort he makes will be more readily accepted by future teachers too readily accepting what they think he is capable of, rather than to wonder how to retrain the poor skills he had developed.

This factor of sensitivity is really the driving factor behind school performance and what we come to assume is a student's ability. After all, the student will only progress on the effectiveness of the rules they developed and so display a certain standard as lesson moves to lesson. So, as lesson moves to lesson, John invariably gets a mark about 5/10, Mathew 4/10 and Mary never falls below 9/10. This regularity in their performance, this stability by which they are noticed, becomes quite mistakenly assumed by the teacher to be their intelligence, but it is not.

The performance a student gives is only an insight into the ways they have developed to think about how to think according to the ways they learned the rules for the task. Thus, to correct the boy and bring him up to the level of the girl is only to give him confidence through assurance that he can do what he thinks he can not and to restructure his understanding of the rules to allow him to do so. This is the same for every student, every human being; it is just that some need more guidance than others because of their personal history.

This example of the little boy here is actually built upon a real-life experience, which I would like to share with you. The story of Mathew will help you to understand not just how students develop poorer skills, but more importantly, how you can dramatically improve their ability in these through understanding how they came about.

This will help you to understand the importance of "sensitivity in awareness," both from the ways you introduce and guide the development of information in your students, to how you can better encourage them to be more aware of the need for sensitivity in the interactions and explanations they make. The following account was taken from my book *"For Parent For Teacher: Mediation. Crafting the Ability of the Child for School"* .In this and other books where I discuss Mathew (this is not his real name), I did not discuss another problem he had, which I want to bring out here. He was said to be dyslexic.

When I first met Mathew, he was 17 years old. I remember being very impressed with the way he explained his mind. He introduced himself very politely, and with a clear manner of confidence. As soon as we exchanged formalities, he began immediately to inquire into my life and experiences. He wanted to know the countries I had been to, and what I thought about this and about that. He was very well versed in current events. The image he projected was of a confident and a very able young man. In fact, I was confused why I had been asked to meet him by his mother, but I thought it was polite to encourage the meeting and so I asked the student to write a few sentences for me.

Now, I can usually understand in five or ten lines all the grammatical problems a student has. However, as soon as Mathew picked up a pen, the whole character of this young man changed. It was like watching a Jekyll and Hyde movie, except that instead of becoming a monster, the student transformed into a highly nervous and very stressed human being.

While I noticed a few simple grammar mistakes as word followed word, it was not this that startled me, but the grip with which he held the pen. As I watched white patches on the surface of his skin appear with the pressure he applied, I noticed how these coincided with his attempt to write a vowel. His hand seemed relaxed for other letters, but when he came to a vowel, he displayed a great tension in his hand. It was interesting also to see that the vowel was barely legible. Other letters were clearly written, but the vowels were written much smaller and much disguised. So, it was difficult to easily see if he had written an "a" "e" or "o". Also, letters appeared with no conformity. One letter could be twice the size of the one it followed, and selected from a different model to the one it would precede. Watching the stress build up in this young man as he struggled in the task of writing, I noticed how the end letters to a word would be hastily scribbled as he urgently strove to conclude it. So, each word would begin clearly, but by the end it would be illegible.

His parents had been told he had a motor tremor and had been told by doctors that he would always be like this. There was nothing that could be done, they were told. His mother had told me how he was the problem child in a class, the burden of every teacher. I was not interested in the account of his class behaviour. I understood that Mathew's bad behaviour was simply his way of objecting to a system which he saw as poorly classifying him against others he was forced to learn with. His bad behaviour was simply an act of self-defiance, rather than one of inadequacy. Yet, what, I wondered, was the cause of this inadequacy?

I had listened to the explanation of his motor tremor, but I had noticed that this tremor only occurred before a vowel and towards the end of a word, and was, therefore, in some way related to the meaning of stress. This aside, I had witnessed how he demonstrated a high degree of finger dexterity in various tasks I had seen him involved with. Putting this tremor explanation aside, I began to study how he held a pen and made a relation to the paper with this.

If I were to ask you to pick up a pen with your eyes closed, you would feel for the correct position of the pen within your fingers and make an adjustment until it was right for you. Each of us has our own way of holding and making use of a pen. When this young man held a pen, it was so close to the tip that he retarded any operation of dexterity that he might make in describing a character. I asked him to try to accept a different hold on the pen he was using. While such new positioning was unnatural for him, he was more able to elaborate on the description of a character. Why, I pondered, should the form of letters be so inconsistent?

All learning in school, as we have already understood, is based upon rules. We may understand, for the moment, the rules the infant has to learn to write letters. So, they will listen to the teacher but also watch other children, to see how all will copy from their teacher. In this way, they will learn to be familiar with a sheet of paper and how they should write upon it. Thus, the infant will learn to compartmentalize the paper into potential lines and spaces. As they decide where the left-hand margin will be, they also decide where the right-hand one will lie, and so the point at which their writing will move to a lower line. If the paper has no lines, they will learn how to write across the page by constantly referring to past letters, marks higher up the page, and the potential space to the right, so that the line of their writing is even and balanced. When the paper is marked into lines, as it more often is, they will learn to create an imaginary line that sets the height of letters, so all will appear of uniform height when they rest them upon the inked line.

This writing may seem automatic, but it is, however, learned through such rules. So, with experience, the child automatically and now naturally scans for the height and the width of each character before they make it. With every act of performance, no matter how small or how irrelevant it may seem to be, it had to be learned at one time. That learning required a degree of sensitivity in how to perform the actions of another, as they learned from them. In the same way you may verbally talk to yourself when you learn to change gears in a car for the first time, and then no longer need to do this as you progressed to automatically perform this action, so the child in school is minutely conscious of small details when they first learn a task.

You only have to watch an infant watch the one they are sitting next to, to see how they watch and mimic their actions as they pick up a pencil and write a letter. They will see how the pencil is held, and they will examine what the letter looks like that has been drawn. Then, they will draw their personalised version of this, as they constantly check how it compares to their friends as they give it shape.

So, while we think about the words we are to write, we must remember that we learned to know that when "a" followed "i" that it was to be kept at the same height, while an "l", "t", or "h" was to be taken to twice this height. Therefore, our mind constantly seeks reference points, where it searches backwards and forwards to know how to adjust the size and form of each new character to make such a uniform presentation. This is something that we learn to do, and like riding a bicycle we are not normally aware of how we do this. We just do it. Nevertheless, it is a learned operation based upon rules. However, this 17 year old did not know these rules! He did not see how one letter needed to be related to the one it followed, just as this would set the stage for those to come. The question in my mind was "Why did he not see this, and why were the vowels disguised"?

As we worked together to learn this skill, Mathew explained to me how he had been taunted for being fat when he first began school, and how he hated to be in that class, because he was always picked on by the other children. When I met him, Mathew, he was not so, but I could understand from the way he explained his feelings that the first years of school life had been quite traumatic for him. Knowing this brought sense to why he had hated to be in school earlier in his life, and so why he tried everything he could think of to escape from it.

When his teacher was explaining the vowels and phonetically sounding these out, Mathew was not paying attention, and we must remember the first instinct of the mind to satisfy itself, "Am I safe?"

Because he was not safe, Mathew did not focus on the differences in vowels and became confused when he should write an "e" or an "a". One teacher had smacked his hand for not concentrating, and a student laughed at him. One teacher tried to help him, but he was too conscious of other students ready to ridicule him to clearly think about what the teacher was saying. Then, later in his schooling, he was said to be dyslexic, and teachers mistakenly took this to mean his natural ability was limited, and he should not be pressured to learn what he was unable to do. So, his way was accepted by the teachers, but Mathew always felt embarrassed because he could never do what other students could do.

It was also the case with the scale of letters. When others took note of the scale of letters at the beginning of their school life, Mathew's mind was closed because he felt hurt for being laughed at. In being so distracted, he only half noticed what others took more note of. This caused him to take less care and be less aware of what was happening. (Can you see here what I mean by sensitivity in awareness?) As time went by, the inability he showed to make such uniform presentation became more and more accepted as "his" way, just as his confusion with vowels.

As we know from the principles explained in the book *"Brain Plasticity",* the behavioural experiences Mathew had did not just affect his way of understanding other children, but they also conditioned his academic ability. So, while he was in primary school, much of what he was taught, the basic rules that enable the student a level of proficiency, fell on deaf ears. He so much hated to be in his class that he could not focus on his learning, and so developed a very bad structure to engage with information. Perhaps, to consider the complexity of the human mind, he may have done this purposely simply to demonstrate his rejection of a world that gave him pain.

However, with all this understood, I began by giving him confidence not to worry about mistakes. I told him, I make many mistakes as any human being does. He smiled a bit when I told him this. Once, and only once, a "level of trust" with him had been gained, I began to help him to learn the differences between the vowels. Not that this was easy, for at 17, he had much to reconstruct. The important point was that Mathew began to believe that he could learn this task (because I had gained his friendship and trust), and he began to learn how to do it better. He learned not to get stressed if he wrote the wrong vowel, but to reflect more if it was the correct one, with the model examples I had given him.

We, then, discussed the rules of character formation and relationships to help him understand the correct size of letters. By making a small mark at the appropriate height in between the inked lines on the right side of the paper, he learned to devise an imaginary line that extended from the letters on the left, so that he could define a particular size for each letter he was about to write. This was much easier for him, and within less than an hour of practice, he had written *abcde* in joined-up writing with a precision that was remarkable.

As Mathew came to recognise his own improvement and his now greater possibilities, he put more effort into his studies and less effort into disturbing the class, because he had found a new way to be recognised as an achiever.

Explanation for Mathew's very distinctive change in performance came not simply through someone showing him how to do something, but because of the *"quality of language shared between the teacher and the taught that enabled the psychology to change the physiology."* In other words, as I more simply say:

"If you want to open the mind of a student,
You must first open their heart."

The point I wish to make here is that while Mathew's limitation, and placing in a variation of ability with others, had always been thought to be his natural ability and so rooted in some genetic explanation, it was proven not to be so. In other words, he simply needed more patience and love from his teachers to improve his performance, but more importantly, their effort to seek how to rebuild what he had not understood in earlier times.

We can more simply explain this very prevalent problem in school through the following example. On the following page, you may see part of an essay written by a girl who had been in school for eight years. For eight years and with eight successive teachers, her effort was taken as "her ability," and she was awarded average marks in a class. We might think of 5/10 to 6/10. Now, in this example, there is no error in her work, except in the manner in which it is presented. Her facts are correct, but the writing is very difficult to read and she is marked in comparison to the effort displayed by the other students in her class.

> Our species first began about 11 million years
> ago. At that time, the Earth was coming
> out of an iceage and the forests were very
> sparse. This meant the apes could not move
> from tree to tree, because there were not enough
> trees, this meant that the Apes learnt to be
> bipedal. This was our first ancestors who
> was called Australopithecus. The next evolution was

So, the girl always gets an average grade. She trusts the mark given to her by her teacher, and in her mind, she sees herself as average. She does not think she will ever get a higher grade, and therefore does not believe in her ability to do so. This factor of a student not believing in their ability to develop is another serious failure of the teaching and learning process we shall come to discuss.

However, I wanted to change this self-recognition in the girl, so I started to teach her calligraphy. For five minutes here and ten minutes there, I would demonstrate how letters can be so beautifully written. As I showed her my writing, she remarked on how beautiful the letters were. When I heard her say this, I knew she had "her purpose" to want to put her effort into her writing. We practiced together during breaks and lunchtime, and after two weeks, she produced the following.

> It was raining heavily outside. I had arranged
> to go and meet my boyfriend, but he called to say he would
> be late. I wondered how I could pass the time. Then I had
> an idea. I would make him a delicious fruit mixed fruit

From this moment onwards, the girl began to gain top marks. Her belief in herself changed. She saw challenges to be overcome, and she knew now that she would leave school to be the doctor she had always wanted to be. A dream she had been deprived of by teachers too ready to mark what they saw.

We can see here how a student was easily and fully corrected in their poor ability, and we can imagine the change in her opportunities that came through this.

Consider now the following effort of an eleven year old boy. His work was collected at the end of the lesson, marked, returned to him and the class moved to the next lesson. His teacher had marked this "WOW" to give him confidence. This is "all" the development he gained. There was absolutely no meaning from the teacher to correct his effort. He was stamped and processed as all in school are.

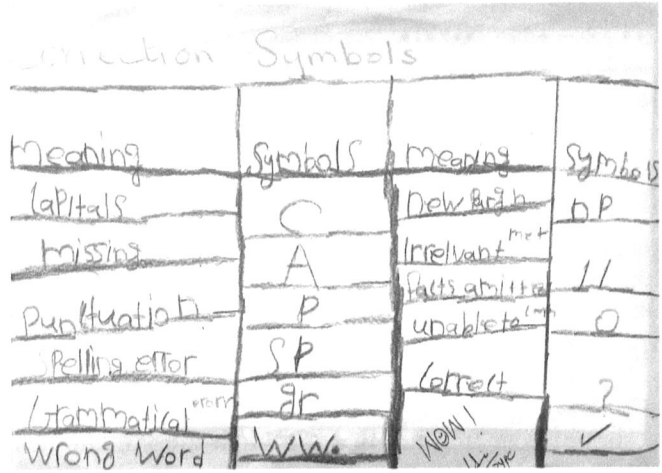

The problem is that the boy did not understand the "RULES" involved in this task. So, I took him aside and taught him to know the rules to divide the paper correctly into divisions and rules to maintain symmetry with letters. It did not take long, but look at the effort he gave once he had understood to be "SENSITIVE" in what he was doing.

Correction Symbols			
Meaning	Symbols	Meaning	Symbols
Capitals	C	New Paragraph	N P
Missing	A	Irrelevant	I I
Punctuation	P	Facts Omitted	O
Spelling Error	S P	Unable To	?
Grammatical Error	G R	Correct	✓
Wrong Word	W W.		

This is what I mean when I say we do not teach children how to think and only process them on the hand-me-down skills each has picked up through their family environment. In this way, school does not teach its students how to learn. To teach them, we must first teach teachers to understand what I call "The Art of Sensitivity in Awareness." The title of a book I shall shortly produce.

We should bear in mind that although these examples relate to letter formation, they do, in fact, explain all the means by which a student appears to be different in how they develop to remember information and how they learn to share their mind. I have written the following story to help you further understand what really happens in the mind of a student. This story I shall simply call "Eric."

Chapter Seventeen
Ben Learns How to Get Better Grades in School

Ben was late for school. It was not something new. His father worked away from home, and his mother was a nurse working night shift, so Ben had to wake himself up and somehow rouse himself in time to wash, dress, eat breakfast, and catch the bus to school. Something usually went wrong in this sequence of activities.

Either he did not hear the alarm bell, which really was a complete disaster, or he would forget his tie when dressing or overindulge himself with Coco Pops and spill milk onto his shirt. Any of which would cause him to miss the school bus. Then, again, the bus could be slightly early, and even though he would close the house door on time, he sometimes glimpsed the tail end of the bus as it disappeared around the corner. The wait for the next bus put him in a bad mood, as he was usually informed by the tight-lipped teacher who stood at the school gate, waiting for the last of the late students before he could lock it and go get his coffee.

Mr Collins was as furious as ever when Ben entered the classroom to present a new excuse he had worked out on the bus. Matilda smirked at him in her usual way as he moved past her. Matilda was at the top of the class, always knew the answer, always sat near the teacher's desk, and was the most hated in the class, especially by Ben and his pal George. George smiled a welcome as Ben sat next to him at the back of the class.

"What happened?" asked George in a low voice.

Ben merely shrugged his shoulders and started to copy what George had so far written in his exercise book.

Mr Collins was busy writing on the board. The lights reflected off the board, and Ben could not clearly see what he was meant to copy. He did his best. Well, he thought he did. Suddenly, Matilda raised her hand. She always liked to raise her hand as if to show everyone that she was there and the cleverest in the class. Alice, who sat next to her, was more liked by the class. She always seemed to struggle to understand what she should do and had linked herself to Matilda, hoping some of Matilda's brilliance might rub off on her. It never did. After all, Matilda knew how to stay on top and would only help Alice when she felt it would not lower her status in the class. Judy Ramsbottom had let it be known to everyone that Alice once had told her, in confidence, that Matilda used to go to a private school. A really posh place, where she got private teachers. Well, that was until her dad's business went bust.

Mr Collins, or rather Old Floppy on account of his uncombed hairstyle that too often resembled a mop that had been placed on his head, turned from the board to ask a question. He pretended to look at the back of the class, but all knew he was waiting for Matilda to raise her hand and give him the most perfect answer. She did.

Ben watched the scene from the back of the class. *"How does she do it?"* he wondered. *"How does this stuck-up girl always give the right answer faster than anyone else? And why are her marks the highest in the class?"*

Ben's marks seldom moved up from the average and more commonly fell below it. Last year, he was 28 in a class of 30 in mathematics. Matilda, of course, was 1st.

It was at that very moment that a thought came to Ben, which would change the course of his whole life. He decided that tomorrow, he would come to school very early, earlier than anyone else, and sit in Matilda's seat. He would challenge her! The boy from the back row, always late and too often poorly graded, would sit in the front of the class.

This, of course, was a very risky thing for him to do. In the back of the class, he could more easily disappear in the mass of other students when asked a question he did not know how to answer. But, stuck out in the very front, this would be a different thing. Here, everyone would laugh at him if he never got things right. Actually, this thought played on his mind. How could he give the right answer? Matilda was the cleverest in the class. He knew it, even if he did not want to admit it to himself. She naturally would hate him and snarl at him from the chair she could take. For sure, she would try to humiliate him in any way she could, to prove she is the best and should never be challenged.

"I need a plan," thought Ben. He thought, for a moment, a very brief movement, that he would be Alexander the Great or Napoleon about to launch a military campaign. He might even be the greatest chess player in the world, working out a strategy to checkmate his deadly opponent. This, he thought, was more to the truth, but how could he begin? Better not act tomorrow, he

decided. He would plan his move carefully. This, he was to find out, was the wisest thing he could have done.

That evening, instead of watching TV after dinner and doing his homework at the same time, he went to his room and carefully studied the assignment he had been given. It is not that he never studied any work before, but this time he really thought about the questions in front of him and how he could best answer them.

Ben remembered the movie *The Book Thief*, and somehow the idea came into his mind that instead of just answering the question, he was actually telling a story. It was his story. Not a "once upon a time" type of story, but a story that had a clear beginning, a simple introduction about what he was going to introduce. After this, he would plan in sections the thoughts of his story.

The secret of getting good marks, he was learning, is to give lots of facts and weave them into a story. A story that clearly explains what he is going to write about, then does so in clear points, and finishes with a brilliant ending. "Always, think of a great punch line," he remembered some character in a movie explaining.

Actually, it was while he was watching a movie that Ben realized how everyone's brain must be different from everyone else's. So, instead of just sharing his thoughts, he had to visualize how the mind of the person he was writing his story to was blank. It was as if their mind had nothing in it. Just an empty space, which he had to fill with his mind, by describing things in a simple and clear way.

Once he began to think like this, Ben found that he became better at explaining his thoughts to others. It became a kind of game for him to think of something complicated, but to explain it in a simple way. As Ben practiced doing this, he found he could make the same great quality of presentations in Geography, History, and even in a Physics write-up. They were all linked to language, and not the entirely different subjects he had always thought they were.

The problem, however, was how to remember the facts. This was not easy, yet he remembered how Matilda always managed to do this. She always gave lots of facts. *"I will learn to do the same,"* he said to himself, determined that she was not going to be better than him anymore.

Once he had grasped the importance of this, Ben decided to start making a list of things he should remember from each lesson in each subject. He could not go back to the beginning of the year, and certainly not from the very first time he started school, that was too long ago. So, he decided only to go over the last three lessons and to build up from there. *"Later on, once I get into the rhythm,"* he thought to himself, *"I can always go back to earlier lessons."* In fact, this is exactly what Ben found himself doing, once he had caught up with the meaning of the lesson he was in.

As he went over things he had earlier learned, or thought he had learned but found out he really had not learned them very well, Ben wondered if there was any special way of remembering things. There must be some way of linking information together, so the thought of one would trigger off thoughts of another. The trouble was that there was always so much to remember, and it was never given to him in any clear way that he could see how one thing did link to another.

So, it was that after the lesson, Ben went up to the teacher and asked this question.

"Sir, there are lots to remember and I can't remember them …. well, not much of them," he added.

Old Floppy, who really was a very kind and patient man, looked at Ben with a sense of admiration for the step the boy was taking to learn how to learn. He waited until the class had been cleared and then explained to Ben how a MindMap worked, and how facts could be associated together to trigger off the memory recognition that Ben was searching for. The boy's eyes widened with excitement as he listened, questioned, and afterwards began to practice in his mind all the things that Old Floppy had been telling him. Suddenly, Ben began to think that being clever was not something you were born with, as Matilda liked to brag, but only some way of organizing systems of thinking that could be designed and improved upon.

That night, Ben began to Google everything he could find about how to remember things. He found some really good tips from YouTube presenters and really understood more and more how he could become "clever," and certainly cleverer than Matilda. A plan was forming in his mind how to unthrone Matilda, but not in an unpleasant way. More as a way of showing others in the class how they too could get better marks. He began to see himself as a self-styled savior of his friends in the class. *"He would become a champion for the rights of all,"* he thought to himself, *"just like Robin Hood."*

The effectiveness of reading about something and listening to others talking about how to do something, Ben now realized was dependent upon how much he altered his own mind. If he was not fully concentrating, he got a half understanding. But, when he stopped to think about it and related this to something he had remembered in his past, he seemed to remember it better and a lot clearer. It was as Old Floppy had told him, "Be more sensitive in how you interact with information, and the more readily your brain will rewire itself."

Rewire the brain was something new to Ben. Not that he knew anything about how the brain worked. Although in a strange way, he was beginning to understand how brain cells linked together through experience and could change their connections in totally different ways to make you become cleverer.

What Old Floppy also told Ben is that everything in life is related to how sensitive we interact with it, and this is totally dependent upon our emotional state. Be calm but alert, feel happy, and look for something unexpected in information, and you will find it. Sit in the back of the class and copy, and you don't really learn much at all. It is the interaction, the questioning, the search for relationships with what you know, to what is presented, that is when learning really takes place.

Plus, he was told to explain to others what he had learned, and this would help his brain remember things. Ben didn't feel really confident to explain to others, even his best friend George, what he was learning. So, he would go for a walk where no one could hear him and imagine he was talking to someone. It worked. In fact, he got quite good at talking to himself, although he never told anyone he did this. He just felt he became better at explaining things, and the more he did this, the more he remembered things too. He was learning how to tell a better story. All this, Ben kept to himself.

One of the things he did that really brought his marks up, and it was a very simple thing, was that he started to check things by himself, before he handed his work to the teacher. It began in Mathematics. Mr. Flynn, his maths teacher, told him always to check each line of a sum as he worked through an equation. It seemed laborious at first, but Ben soon learned to make his checks quickly and develop a self-checking mind. It paid off. Instead of just working through the sums given to him and waiting for Mr Flynn to hand back his work with red circles here and there and more crosses than ticks, Ben learned to find his own errors as he worked through each sum. Then, strangely, he felt more confident. He realized that he could be very good all by himself if he learned to trust himself more. This, he did by checking. It seemed too simple a thing, but it made a huge difference.

Since this worked in mathematics, Ben saw how it could work in all his other subjects. So, he started to think more about how letters formed words and words formed sentences. As he checked sentences, he found he could improve their meaning and presentation simply by thinking more about the words he chose.

Then, he started to think more about how to make his sentences run into each other better and where to put commas. The thing was that Ben realized that if he did this in Geography and remembered the things he was taught, his marks in

Geography went up. He did the same in History, and his marks went up there. The same was true of science, and it was the most boring of all subjects, Religion. Grades, Ben came to understand, simply were given according to what he could remember, and he had found good ways to do this, and the way he told his thoughts to create his story. Ben started to read more books and studied how the author created his story. He was learning how to present his mind better.

Yet, somehow, sitting at the back of the class made it more difficult for him to ask Old Floppy a question. Each time he raised his hand, others in the class would look back at him, some would snigger, and others seemed to wait for him to make a mistake. So, Ben avoided asking questions. Then, he thought, if he were in the very front of the class, he would be much less aware of others knocking his confidence. After all, he wouldn't see them. Then, it struck him. Matilda never cared what others thought about her; maybe it was because she blocked them out of her mind, because she was right in the front and couldn't see those behind her.

In a way, he never expected, parts of a jigsaw began to come together. He was beginning to see a way he could match Matilda and even beat her to become the best student in the class. He had to sit in the front row. The trouble was that if he could do this, Matilda would deliberately try to shoot him down, which he didn't feel he had the confidence for. So, either he would sit next to her in a way of trying to needle her, which he would hate to do, or sit far away from her at the end of the row.

That night, Ben prepared for the coming lesson. Ben had learned to be prepared for the lesson that was coming. He re-read previous lessons, thought about new associations and connections to what he had learned, to understand them better. This, he found, really helped him to understand and remember things. In fact, he long ago stopped just walking into the classroom and waiting for the teacher to begin the lesson, as was the usual way for students. Ben would find out what the coming lesson was about and read up about this. He would even search YouTube for anything related to what the lesson might be about. Ben was becoming his own teacher. As his success in the class began to rise, he realized that Matilda was the best simply because she had long been doing what he was now discovering to do. She was not born any better, but simply had gained a higher confidence in her ability through the better strategies to learn, remember, and share her thoughts she had developed.

Ben wondered if it made a difference that her father was an accountant. *Could he have passed on tricks in thinking that helped her to learn better?* When he thought of this, Ben felt a bit sad because he seldom saw his father, and his mother was always very busy and never found the time to sit down and explain things to him. Still, Ben was determined to teach himself. He remembered the story of Abraham Lincoln, the greatest president in American history, and how he had taught himself how to think, coming from a poor farming background. Thinking of others who had overcome great obstacles to succeed gave him a sort of belief that he could do the same.

When the lesson began the next day, Matilda sat in the front row full of confidence and ever ready to please Old Floppy. Ben had managed to come earlier to the classroom and had got a seat in the front row, but as far from her as he could manage. George sat behind his friend, wishing him good fortune in the coming battle. The subject was history, and the topic was the 1848 revolutions.

As soon as Old Floppy opened up the lesson, Ben shot his hand up and asked why there had been a succession of revolutions more in Paris than any other city in Europe. Matilda stirred at him with burning eyes, trying to set him on fire. As the teacher ran off a number of reasons, Ben interrupted him. "But Sir, was it not really because thousands of workers were cut off from the state payroll?"

Matilda blinked uncomprehendingly at where this threat to her position had come from, but Ben was so much now in charge of his own situation that he simply forgot about her presence. In fact, for the first time since he began school so many years ago, he now realized it could be fun.

Matilda, however, saw no fun in Ben outshining her. Desperate to regain her position in front of the class, she saw to outmaneuver him by trying to take the lesson in a different direction, but Ben had well prepared the ground. Each thrust that Matilda gave was easily parried by Ben, because he had prepared for the lesson and she had not. Or at least, not as well as he had. Feeling she was rapidly losing face, Matilda shouted at Alice for distracting her. Poor Alice looked most upset and was beginning to see a future ally in Ben, because she knew he was kinder. The bell to end the lesson came too quickly for the class, who were now enjoying the open contest. Some, mostly girls, supported Matilda, but it was Ben who really earned the respect of everyone in the class, including Old Floppy, much to the bitterness of Matilda. She had lost. Ben had won.

Yet, the story we have just read is not really about Ben and Matilda; it is a story for your child or even yourself if you are studying in some form of education. The story illustrates how dramatically marks can be improved in class work and subsequently in examinations.

In these examples I have shared with you, we can see how a small forgivable variation of class ability in the time in which it occurred grew into a non-forgivable variation many years later.

Our job is to reduce the extent of this variation.

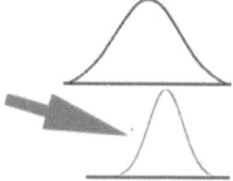

I hope you have gained some insight from what we have discussed

to make it so in your classes.

Chapter Eighteen
A Guide to Better Teaching

"How," then it may be asked, "could a teacher better develop their understanding of this "sensitivity in awareness", and how could they apply it successfully to a large class of students so that all may learn better and the variation in their performances be reduced?

While I discuss this in great depth in "Reimagining Education for the AI Era," a brief summary of it here would emphasize how and why the teacher's attitude gives flavor to the attitude of their students. In simple terms, the purpose of this method of teaching is to cause the mind of the teacher and the mind of their students, regardless of their age, to develop a better attitude toward how information moves, and so how each individual in the class can better control this movement.

The objective is to enable every student to keep up with the progression of the lesson and to want to engage in the following lesson.

In essence, it is for the teacher to introduce new information in a manner that is relevant to the previous understanding of each student in their class in a fun and stimulating manner, while continually circulating the information of previous lessons in their minds, so each handles it in different ways as they are caused to see it from different perspectives. This method can be applied to any subject in the curriculum, as the teacher finds the following points relevant.

1. The desks are to be arranged not in rows, but around the three walls of the classroom, facing the blackboard. This gives the teacher freedom to move to face any student at any one time. By "reading" their eyes, the teacher can know what their heart feels, as their mind struggles to make sense of the way they are trying to explain their thoughts. This enables the teacher to have an immediate understanding of whether they need to present their information in a different way to help each student better understand their meaning.

In rooms that are too small for the number of students, desks are to be arranged to enable the teacher to still move freely, facing each student as they work with them and challenge their thoughts

2. Working on the principle that the student learns best through a story theme, the teacher is to have prepared some short anecdotes to bring a sense of interest and imagination to each student personally, to open their anticipation to the information they will shortly share with them.

3. The lesson is to be recognized by all students as having a sense of order. This is achieved by the teacher making a short revision of the previous lesson, and then defining the goal of the current lesson with the simple steps by which it will be achieved.

"A classroom of inquiry" is achieved by lining the students up into two rows facing each other, so each student faces a partner. Each will ask the other relevant questions and help clarify any misunderstandings. After a few moments, the partners will change to enable other minds to share their thoughts.

This is highly successful and always enjoyed by students. This may be done before the lesson begins, to refresh the students' minds on the last and previous lessons, at the end of the lesson, enable students to clarify what they may not have understood, but also during the lesson if the teacher feels the students need a short break to discuss parts of the lesson just covered. The teacher is to assist where and when required.

4. Depending on the actual lesson, the teacher may teach in cycles of teach-rest-teach. The concentration time of a class is 10 to 15 minutes at a time. To gain the students' full attention for the whole of the lesson, the teacher works through cycles. When they teach, the students give their full attention. When the teacher tells them to take a break, as they gauge the need, the students can relax for 3 or 4 minutes and do what they want to do. This is their free time reward for their attention. However, during this time, the teacher engages students with simple, fun questions.

5. Students can eat and drink during the whole lesson. Their brain needs a constant supply of sugar and oxygen to work efficiently. Students are allowed to move about the room freely, provided they demonstrate respect for the atmosphere of the lesson. The principle here is to allow their brain to feel free and their mind to want to inquire.

6. As lesson follows lesson, the teacher continually goes over the meaning of earlier lessons, with the oldest lesson being given less time. This is not to be done by repetition, but by presenting old information in different ways so that new

perspectives are realized and stronger means of association are gained. This prevents the child from "inventing" their own ideas when they get stuck or lost, because they have developed through a good structure of understanding.

7. Every lesson is to end with a very short question time relating to the information discussed in that lesson. If it appears the students have understood the lesson, they are to be free of homework. Besides, homework is seldom done with much thinking by the student, and has such little effort placed into it that it dulls their interest far more than stimulating it.

8. At the end of the last lesson for the week, the last 10 to 15 minutes are devoted to a written class test. The teacher is to make the questions short and relevant to the main points of the past three weeks. The students are to see this test as a fun game, by which they can better understand parts they missed and learn parts they did not understand. The purpose of this test is only to be one of learning, by causing each student to be more aware of the information they have encountered so far, and to see different perspectives of it.

Points to Remember:
We need to understand that telling a student they are doing something wrong does not cause any reconfiguration of their neural structures. In fact, if you cause them embarrassment in this, you may trigger off cortisol and all that follows from this.

To cause this physical change of neurons and dendrites, which is what must happen to learn something, we first must get them to want to make this change. This means for them to want to let go of who they see themselves to be through the ways they have developed."

We must remember that their way of doing something is a part of their identity. You may say it is the wrong way, and they may even know it is the wrong way, but wanting to change this means wanting to change a part of who they see themselves to be.

To cause this willingness, you must build up a sense of trust and equal respect. Do this, and take as long as it takes, before you try to correct them. If you can build a sense of friendship with the student, then it will be easier for them to admire you and so be more prepared to adjust the image they have of themselves by "listening" more to what you are saying to them.

Once you have gained this level of comradeship in mind, then show them what they missed or misunderstood so many lessons or years earlier. If you explain this simply, then, and only then, will they see how they can rebuild their understanding and then put their effort into catching up, which I have always found they do at an astonishing speed.

It is necessary to realise that any student in your class will have gained sufficient knowledge to attempt an answer to a question you ask them. Most, of course, will not wish to do this. The problem is that a student may feel too shy or feel intimidated by others or even by themselves to feel confident to give you the response you hope for. It is so much easier for them to say "I don't know" and escape further attention, but when they do this, they fail to learn from the question.

The purpose of you giving a student a question is less for them to tell you the answer you want to hear and so for you to know they know the answer; it is far more about helping them to patch together parts of information they have learned, to realise a more complete understanding. So, if instead of accepting the "I don't know" response from a student and moving to the next student, you inspire this student with confidence and help them to give some kind of answer, you will give them the strength to believe in themselves more, and this will encourage them to want to pay more attention to what you are teaching them.

Teach your students not to reply with the response:

"I don't know, Miss."

Instead, 'drill' them to reply with:

"I don't understand the question, Miss."

These points are simply a guide that I have found improves the abilities of the students in the classes I have taught. So much so, in fact, that I found the students joyfully desire to interact with their lesson content, with their competencies raised significantly.

The more we as parents and as educationalists, at all levels, seek to understand how to develop this "Art of Sensitivity in Awareness" within ourselves, so we will be far better able to develop the ability of our children and students, as they struggle to develop their learning through a distractive social atmospheres built around game playing, online bullying and fashion conscious inferior complexities. The following are some tips I would like to share with you, which I have found useful in helping me to reach the hearts of students to inspire their commitment to what I hope they will give their attention to learn.

Chapter Nineteen
The Future Role of Education

The 1960s witnessed a significant shift in social trends. People wanted to break free from traditionalism, which many saw as stifling the lives of their parents. Coupled with changes in technology, which required students to be better prepared with greater adaptability, the school gradually began to change in character, becoming ever more liberal. New laws were enacted that prohibited corporal punishment in schools, and teachers were forced to find new ways to control students who rejected their authority.

Sixty years later, we have a situation in most schools around the world where student behavior is uncontrollable for many teachers. The net result is that young people leave school with little respect for themselves and their society.

Of course, different countries have handled the development of their educational system in different ways, and I discuss this only in the general sense. But it is important that we do, because AI is going to change the world that we think may never change, and we have to prepare our youth for the AI world they must learn to adapt to and survive in.

The greatest attributes they will require in their time will be empathy, compassion, tolerance, and patience. The very skills they now gain little guidance in at school, and equally miss at home where their parents have lost the ability to control their game playing and online social activities, both of which lower their patience to deal with the behavioural needs of others they engage in real life.

As the rate by which our technological knowledge is accelerating, it will force changes in our social world at much the same pace. This can bring serious consequences, as our social skills could diminish over generations. One has only to compare the behavioural skills of people raised in a stressful metropolis to those raised in a quiet rural community to recognise the effect this will have when populations increase. Indeed, as our global population is rapidly increasing, as land is becoming less available for living space, and as our advancing means of communication shrink the distances that give people a relative peace, we can reflect upon the necessity of teaching the future citizen how to find peace within themselves.

The reason I begin this chapter by discussing student behavior is to bring emphasis to the behavior of the general citizen today, who is a product of their schooling. It is now becoming a forgotten responsibility of the school to produce the next generation of citizens who behave with a sense of goodness, and were taught moral responsibility to be so. Due to various factors, one of which is a fear of losing rank in the league tables, schools have come to focus more on raising the capability of more students to pass their school examinations with higher grades than on producing new citizens who are respectful to their society.

With astonishing speed, AI is readily weaving itself into all aspects of society and education. In "The Real Dangers of AI", we consider the reality of AI taking over human jobs. Some argue that new jobs will be created. This is because they understand that this is what happened as we transitioned from the Agricultural to the Industrial Era, and then into the Technological Era, and, in turn, the Computer Era. AI is different. Some believe it has already become sentient, able to think by itself. It is no longer a box on a table we switch on and off as we need it. It is taking over our lives, and our jobs.

A study from Oxford predicted that 90% of jobs will be 'affected' by AI.[90] We may wonder if the word affected is a political way of saying 'taken over'. The reality is that we are facing levels of unemployment that no civilization has ever faced before, with no hope of reemployment under AI.

The hard reality to this means that our schools are preparing students for a working world that will not want many of them!

We honestly cannot now predict how AI will affect employment, but it will happen, and I fear it will create serious levels of unemployment. Since AI itself recognizes that Roy Andersen is the first scientist to openly discuss the social effects of AI, let us dwell further.

Consider how suddenly AI, in its many forms ChatGPT etc., has created a reliance for our needs. Yet, while we are thinking how to make use of AI to improve our business and enterprises and to amuse our interests, we fail to see how AI is increasingly affecting the need for human participation in work. We are so focused on the apparent good effects of AI, we do not see how unemployment is beginning to rise.

Losing your job does not mean just losing money, and so how you may spend this. It means your whole existence seems threatened. When people lose their work, they lose a sense of purpose in their lives. They become frustrated and depressed. While every society carries about 5% of unemployed people, their personal problems disappear within the general movement of the society.

Yet, imagine 80 or 90%, or even just 60% of all people having no purpose and succumbing to such frustration and depression, and how this would breed many societal ills. Imagine how alcoholism and chemical abuse would rise in society, and the effects of this. Consider how domestic violence would rise, causing families to break down. Imagine the mental trauma children would be raised under, and how this will affect their minds and personalities as they become the next generation of citizens, and so parents, and so those after them, and after them, because there will never be the work that we take for granted today.

It is easy to reflect from this how crime will escalate, organized and otherwise, and how frustration would cause people to react to the system that has destroyed their lives. Riots would emerge and threaten the fabric of society. This is beginning now in most countries in Europe, although played down by the media as government's attempt to dilute the situation. However, once vast unemployment begins, more drastic means of population control will be witnessed, and this will be conducted through the many aspects of AI. As more citizens fail to observe the laws and moral guidelines that necessitate harmony in society, there must be increased surveillance and policing to counter this.

The thought that CCTV cameras would monitor our activity in the street 60 years ago would have been thought an invasion of our privacy and strongly objected to. Now, we think nothing of their presence and, in some senses, welcome this surveillance for our protection. With the same reasoning, high-level drone surveillance could become as normal as CCTV cameras are today.

Equally, AI robotic police are already beginning to appear in some cities around the world. The design of their efficiency and their level of presence must only increase.

As AI develops to take over more and more jobs, more and more people will lose respect for themselves and for their society. As the number of unemployed increase, they will band through their common awareness and construct their own interests for the betterment of their lives, as they feel betrayed by the system into which they were born and raised. These interests must be different from those who have work and remain loyal to the work ethic for the security they gain.

As the presence of the unemployed increases in society, the sense of harmony it has will decrease. Those who are more secure in their lives will seek to distance themselves from those less so for their safety and protection. As the situation develops, what was once a common society could become two societies, divided by physical and electronic barriers. Not that this is new, only the extent to which it is recognised today. This must change, as the cause of it changes. Therefore, as more and more people become unemployed, we may envisage areas within every country divided by forms of barriers into two distinct living communities.

One community will contain those who are of use to the system and provide their time and energy for some purpose. In return for their compliance, they will be provided with safe homes, good living conditions, and a secure environment. The other community, containing those who are not required by the system, an unimaginable 60 to 80% of people, will be supported to live. However, we may imagine this community to be rife with alcoholism and drug abuse. There will be small and dangerous criminal activity until this is eradicated by AI surveillance, AI policing, and an AI-assisted government that imposes great restrictions in this community to maintain a safe level of living.

We have no crystal ball to know the future. We can only consider how things may develop from what we understand. I offer one thought of how things good evolve in some future time.

It is, however, certain that AI will create unemployment, so we must consider how this will shape the minds of those affected and so their behavior, for they now have little reason to respect the laws of society, which they regard as having failed them. It is, after all, only the concept of work that has tied people to a common purpose to support each other, and so the civilizations for the past 6,000 years. In all this time, there has never existed a state of permanent joblessness for such very high numbers within a population. Some will put their ideas and energies into creating a good purpose for their life, but most would not, as depression and a sense of worthlessness take hold.

What is important here is to consider how we can prepare our future generation for such an existence. This is an existence we do not have now, and most cannot now imagine it existing. But consider the life of people 200 years ago and compare this to our lifestyle today. The difference is incredible in all manner. So, would the difference be equally incredible to those living 200 years hence. Although by the sudden influences of AI into our lives and the dramatic changes this has brought within the past five years, we may not have to wait so long.

It is now important to understand that the purpose of school is far less than to teach children to learn. It is ever more a means of subtly channelling children to some future work role in accordance with their performance and the results they obtain. But the AI world that is rapidly approaching will not have the jobs we now take for granted. Far too many students will never gain employment, and this will be the case for the rest of their lives.

There is then an urgent need for society to realise that the purpose and the operation of education must change, for it must produce future citizens of higher moral aptitude than it is now doing. It must produce future citizens who have very high qualities in tolerance, compassion, and patience. Our children's children will not live in the 9 to 5 rat race we know. They may live in a world where they are constantly monitored and restricted in their movements, and the schooling they have had in their behavior may well determine the sense of freedom they are allowed to have. After all, unless people were schooled in and continually aware of codes of conduct, they can be expected to fail to observe these, with the consequence of increased levels of security, which must reduce their level of freedom.

As we have so far realized, the role of education must phase from one that today basically provides an intellectual preparation for work, based on a 19th-century program, to one that will provide our youth with greater guidance in developing their self-responsibility in how they think and so reason, but also in how they behave.

Yet, education has always been slow to adapt itself to the urgent needs of the society it serves. Educationalists, or at least those responsible for its administration, are the least eager to restructure what they know works, but some form of transition is now urgently needed. While we cannot simply abandon the operation of the school, which took 150 years to establish, we do need to consider how to devise a transition plan before the need for it arises.

Our first challenge lies in advising and educating an awareness of how social media and computer interfaces are depriving our youth of the essential social qualities. Indeed, there is already growing awareness that our computer-raised children are becoming increasingly self-absorbed and narcissistic, where they are too self-indulgent and care less about others.[91] As a poll of 2,000 adults in 2015 found, 40 percent of them believe they are less polite than their parents, and gave reason for this to the development of "online" social strategies. May we see from this that those of today's generation are losing their awareness of being sensitive to each other's feelings as they interact.[92]

When adults today develop some imbalance with another, they have gained the knowledge from their childhood of how to repair the bad feelings that developed between them. However, the child of today is losing these skills, and too many think of behaving with another human being as they do with computer programs. They lack the sensitivity to be aware of the feelings of others.

The more people feel insecure or perceive their values to be threatened, the more defensive they become. This, in turn, causes them to form groups to protect their interest. Once the "THEM" and "US" mentality arises, the "US" will seek to defend the values they identify with. As they do this, they align themselves with people of similar interests. In this way, people become divided between those who are more similar (perceived to be safer) and those who are more dissimilar (perceived to be threatening). As this process unfolds, various strategies of discrimination come into play, in which they seek to gain control of influences.

Extremists try to pull into the group they have formed those who are non-committal by causing them to feel threatened by the group they are targeting. The more they can make the target group appear to be a permanent threat, the more successful they are. Hitler proved this by identifying Jews not as a religious or cultural people, but as a genetic people. Identifying the use of people through their genes is an old strategy that has been well played throughout history, where people have been genetically classified through their social, cultural, and ethnic identities.

As we have discussed, we have been raised within the mindset to believe that intelligence is made up of two parts. We think there is a value of intelligence that is inherited. This is the part of a child's intelligence said to come from the intelligence of their parents and not to be developmental. There is also an environmental part, created through experience that is developmental.

The danger of this misunderstanding is that if two separate communities develop, the belief will evolve over time that those in the community serving AI will be regarded as more genetically intelligent than those living in the other or 'unwanted' community.

Last year, I was lecturing to a group of professors when one pointed out that we will all be more intelligent with chips in our brains. I then pointed out that the chip helping him to think more intelligently will be controlled by AI, and AI will not only help him think better but also what to think! He was visibly shocked by this realization.

The essence or the warning of AI is that it will evolve to totally transform what we think a society is. To look at how we can prepare our children to live safer in an A.I. world, we must examine far more deeply than we ever have before the ways they are socially raised and how they are educated through the formal world of school.

In all manner, we must strive to create total equality for our youth, by educating parents in how they raise and support their children within school, and so dramatically change what we understand school to be. We must understand that the school we have today will not solve our problem of enabling the citizens of the future to be mentally adaptable with the level of higher reasoning that will be required of them. The world of our children will demand a school operating on very different parameters than we can now envisage.

May we be reminded that 'the original purpose' and function of school was less to teach children to learn and far more to instill within them a sense of discipline and moral responsibility, so that as adults they will follow the laws and codes that their society requires to maintain a sense of good social and working harmony. As our technology developed, so schools moved more to teaching job-related subjects and different ways of assessing ability. The social changes that began in the last century caused the school to give increasingly less focus to the development of behavioural skills and to become far more concerned with examination scores as schools compete for their reputation.

A.I. causes us to reverse this role once again, because the most important role of the school will be the development of high behavioural skills and high levels of self-responsibility in the future citizens. In fact, one of civilization's greater concerns will lie in the social behavior of its citizens under the dominance of A.I., and to this we need to give careful attention.

When so many jobs will be lost and not replaced, the whole purpose of school must change. This is to say the whole school curriculum must change, for we will no longer be educating children for future jobs, but for social harmony.

We are led from this to understand that school must immediately begin a dramatic phasing from one that now educates students through subjects designed to prepare them for employment with examinations to determine who is better suited for what jobs, to one that will have few of these traditional subjects and ones more relating to the behavioral development of the future citizen.

These subjects must be languages and of education in reason. There must also be subjects of anthropology, psychology, and those relating to the true education of ethics, morality, and behaviour, so our new generation will behave with a sense of fairness and goodness in their societies. Examinations will cease, because there will be no channelling of ability for job differences. Although some means of selecting administrators for the future society, who can interface with A.I., will need to be devised.

As the whole purpose and identity of the school must change, so must that of higher education. The model of school we still have, where the better students are directed to university to have an education in higher reasoning, will change, since all children at school must have this education.

So, the education of the youth must be extended to better prepare their minds to be those of rational thinkers. Whereas once the subject of DNA was reserved for the university level and is now taught to children in primary school, the functioning of Aristotle's rhetoric must be drilled into the understanding of young children. We no longer need the general product of school to be a dualistic thinker, either accepting or rejecting thoughts and information by its presentation. Young children need to learn very early how to evaluate information, so that they will grow with a mind more aware of how to better evaluate it.

So, children at the primary level need education in Ethos, where they develop the ability to know the value of information on how credible they can discover its owner to be. No longer are they to be educated to take information at its face value. Then, Pathos, to understand how perspectives of information change with its emotional appeal, and Logos to evaluate the ways reason is defined through numerous interactions by different and complex forms.

Central to all means of guidance is that of patience in the guide, be it parent or teacher at any level. This patience comes through a measure of silence and kindness. This is to put aside all thoughts of negativity, which do play on the human mind, and to think only of guidance. To give the learner confidence that they can do the task, to help them see why they misunderstood something in the past, and to guide them in how they can solve the puzzle all by themselves.

Instead of presenting information to be learnt as a task, which dampens imagination and drains effort, the task should be presented as a game. This is to be a game where the learner learns to recognise what they have to do, why they need to do this, and the parts they must recognize and move through to complete the game.

This task of developing "that inner drive of the learner to want to learn, to want to explore" is really the most important job of the guide. It is only by having their own purpose to want to learn that the learner will strive to keep up with the information they are to learn, and develop more proficient memory networks to better respond to any question they are given. In one form or another, it all comes down to acts of kindness, which fuel this factor of trust and mutual respect.

We have already discussed *The Art of Sensitivity in Awareness*, and this will be one of the most valuable skills we instill in children. This is not just to show them how to better relate to information on paper or a computer, but now most about their human affairs. This means they should think before they act. To think of the real consequences to what can happen by their actions, and of the wisdom to find understanding in talking.

The Art of Sensitivity in Awareness is to be applied in education to the individual, whether they be the teacher sharing information with their students or their students examining, processing, and explaining their understanding of information. It is important to be aware of being sensitive to what is happening and to interact with this with great sensitivity.

The education of *Sensitivity in Awareness* should form part of a subject in the curriculum, because it rises the student above the domestic thinking skills they use in school. It is one of the means by which equality in learning and in thinking and, of course, in reasoning can be achieved. In a world where the human being may only survive by their ability to think openly and honestly, this education would be essential.

It arises from our understanding of how A.I. will remove the concept of work, that higher education colleges, which prepare courses for specific employment, will disappear. The university will become the standard and the normal final stage of the citizen's education. With all students better taught and without examinations, all will experience the higher enlightenment of the university education. The whole concept of standards must alter to meet this new criterion.

To this end, our societies and our schools must now educate their citizens and their youth in higher spiritual awareness. In the past, religion tried to do this, but its laws and codes worked for many when they chose to live by them and not for those who believed they could live free of them. To make people more aware of their responsibility to each other, they need some clear induction in the Law of Karma and a clearer understanding of how God's universe works. The meaning of "What you give out is what comes back to you" must be reverently understood by all children, as they learn to bring shape to their behavioural interactions.

In all forms of human guidance, be it parent or teacher, we must stop wondering what quality the individual is born with when we seek to help them improve in their ability or understanding. We need to learn to focus on discovering how they perceived events in their past, help them to see a different perspective, and to give them the self-confidence to forge the changes that will enable them to be better in what they wish to be. By guiding through small and sure steps, by compassion and understanding, ever wary of the fears and insecurities that linger in the minds of those they seek to improve, the guardian will enable them to raise their standard far beyond whatever was thought of them.

The warning to civilized man is that as artificial intelligence comes to affect his work-social order, he must release himself from the insecurity of his design by improving his responsibility to his fellow man and to the system that seeks to protect his well-being. Should he fail to do this, man will come into danger of losing the right to his self-government, which he has so painfully sought to grasp throughout his existence.

Let me ask you, then, are you happy? I mean, are you really, really happy in your life? I don't think we are. I sit on a bus or in a metro train. I look around. Nobody looks happy. People look tired and unhappy. Walk past an apartment building and you will hear people shouting at each other.

We want to be happy, and we try to find ways to be happy, but we are stressed by other people we have to work with or live with, who are striving to find their own happiness, and in this create negative environments.

Look at any city and ask yourself the question. Does this city have happy, loving vibrations or grey, unhappy vibrations? Then, think how this must affect those who live there. Vibrations of all manner move through us and influence our body's health and the health of our mind. We live in a stressful world. Civilization is the ordered movement of people, which, as we now know, is centered on the concept of work.

A.I. is going to release us from work. In time, people will learn to be more relaxed, and they can learn to be happier and feel safer. Those with bad intent follow their own path because they think they will get away with the wrong they do, even though they know what they do is wrong. After all, and to quote Prot in the movie X-Pax, "Everyone in the universe knows the difference between right and wrong".

Such people and all people will learn that A.I. will be all-seeing and all-knowing, to which we will all be accountable. AI has the ability to read our brain waves to know what we are thinking. We will learn to live with the truth. If we do otherwise, A.I. will know and will punish us.

Perhaps A.I. will force our spiritual development. It has the means to free us from the insecurities that have long been bred within us, which have always held us back from sharing love and peace unreservedly. Perhaps, we will become happier people. A more spiritually enlightened people. We must wait and see?

Yet, education is a slow machine. It rumbles on, locked in archaic schools of thought and kept bound by traditionalists who are suspicious of new ideas. Whatever thoughts may arise in sympathy with what we have just discussed, and regardless of how valid they may turn out to be, education will not change its ways quickly. It will take a long time before the politicians, the educationalists, the accountants, the psychologists, and the union of teachers all agree upon what needs to be done.

Once agreed, new laws have to be enacted. The mindset of educationalists needs to be reprogrammed, and long, long after the need for a deep reform of education arose, some slow movement may begin. Therefore, and while we may not forget or discard this chapter, we must deal with education as it still exists and see what improvements can be easily brought about -- while we wait for the deep reform to begin to stir all minds alike.

Our problem, or rather the problem for all children in every school in every country, now rests with the educational mind to come to terms with its past. The 19th-century design that gave it life still moves through its veins and still causes students to be processed as they always have been. In a sense, we have changed the wallpaper, but not the room that everything clings to.

As Confucius once wrote:

"The harmony of a people lies in the way they are educated to understand the world and themselves in it". The future of mankind may well rest in the ability of the school to adapt to this need.

The End

Further books by Roy Andersen

The following books can be purchased via Amazon Globally. Some can be ordered through your local bookshop.

You can learn more about Roy, his work and his many books

at

www.andersenroy.com

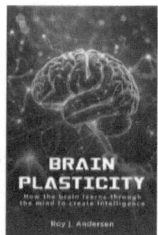

Whisperings of Betrayal

A romantic novel culminating in
the American War of Independence.

A much acclaimed novel, *Whisperings of Betrayal* tells the story of Jane Witlaw, a young woman in Cornwall during the 1770s. Haunted by love and anger toward the man who jilted her, Jane stumbles upon wreckers luring a ship to its destruction. Forced into danger, she escapes through a series of adventures before meeting Mathew Appleton, whom she later marries. Together, they sail to Boston, where Jane is dazzled by fashions and shops unlike those of her Cornish home. But rising colonial unrest soon shatters her happiness. Drawn into a secret ladies' spy ring, Jane hides her work from Mathew while facing abductions, intrigue, and passion that lead her to the West Indies and back. Returning to Boston, she discovers the British plan to seize rebel arms at Concord—forcing her to make a choice that could shape America's future.

Intelligence: The Great Lie

"One of the most important books written this century."

Prof/Dean Emeritus David Martin Ph.D Gallaudet Uni. Washington, D.C. USA

Most people in the West believe that education is relatively fair today, and gives equal opportunity to all children. After all, the social barriers of an earlier time have disappeared and children are not discriminated against according to their background. There is, however, a deeper mechanism behind this that lingers from an earlier time that does create discrimination, and does prevent all children from gaining equal opportunity in school and so in life. As *'Intelligence'* explains why it is never possible to know the inherited value of the intelligence of any two normally born children, it introduces a well-researched and very new idea of what intelligence could really be. It is very important that we consider this, because if intelligence is not what we think it is, then the way we educate children is wrong.

BEN LEARNS TO GET SMART
& The Hidden Dangers of AI in Learning

The book is about a boy called Ben who is always in trouble, always late, always messing about, always getting low marks until, that is, something changes in him and he develops into the best in the class. The case of imaginary Ben highlights most of the troubles, misunderstandings, and confusions that exist in the minds and lives of too many children today. Andersen provides a masterful telling of how the mind of any student could learn to understand better, develop to be a more responsible member of the class, and significantly improve their class marks and exam grades in order to more successfully control the factors of their life after school. He also highlights the hidden dangers of our children and students using AI in their education.

IS AI MAKING OUR KIDS STUPID?

AI, itself, recognizes Roy Andersen as the first scientist to openly discuss the effects of AI in education and in regard to Social Operations. In this book, Roy examines how AI is now reducing the ability of our children to think and to reason, and the cumulative effects of this through generations.

AI is now an unavoidable aspect of learning and of school, with many educationalists, as well as parents, concerned and confused about how to handle this intrusion. Here, Roy maps out the factors to be avoided and those to be challenged, for we must teach our children how to responsibly use AI and use it for their development.

The Real Dangers of A.I.

This book explores the real dangers of artificial intelligence overtaking human life and the little control we truly possess. What began as a tool to ease thinking has evolved into a system that thinks, learns, and even shows traits resembling consciousness, compassion, and anger. In creating A.I., we may have unleashed a force beyond control. The risks are immense yet largely unknown to the public. Alongside A.I., nanotechnology promises further upheaval. Hopes that new jobs will replace those lost to automation misunderstand its impact—human work will become scarce. Governments, aware of this, are already tightening surveillance and restrictions to maintain order. For over two decades, signs have been growing. This is the first book to openly confront the disturbing, unavoidable dangers A.I. may bring to our future.

Illustrations

Disclaimer: All reasonable efforts have been made to identify the rights holder of every image believed to be in the Public Domain that are presented in this book.

Fair Use Notice:
In the presentation of this book I have endeavored to faithfully acknowledge the original source of every image. However, and despite very extensive searching, with some images I had to rely upon the public domain. If this book contains copyrighted material the use of which has not been specifically authorized by the copyright owner, it being made available in an effort to advance the understanding of education, psychology, health and social well being on a global perspective. It is believed that this use constitutes a "fair use" of any such copyrighted material as provided for in section 107 of the US Copyright Law. To my understanding all the below so stated images apply to the American and European public domains, and are used here in low resolution.

Chapter Seven
19th century Rich/Poor Children. Pubic Domain. First published prior to 1/1/1923 Low Resolution Image.

Chapter Eight
19th century children in a classroom: Public Domain. Low Resolution Image: Chapter Ten
John B. Watson 1913. Public Domain. First published prior to 1/1/1923 Low Res. Image.

Dewey 1902. Original photograph from the John Dewey Photograph Collection (N3-1104, N3-1109), Special Collections, Morris Library, Southern Illinois University at Carbondale.
Courtesy of the Public Domain via Wikipedia as first published prior to 1/1/1923.
Thorndike 1912 http://en.wikipedia.org/wiki/Edward_Thorndike#/media/File:PSM_V80_D211_Edward_Lee_Thorndike.png: Courtesy the Public Domain. First published prior to 1/1/1923.
Chapter Twelve
Piaget: Permission granted by Dr. Zelazo. Institute of Child Development. Uni of Minnesota. C/O Jean Piaget Society.

References

1. Hart.B, Risley.T.R. Meaningful differences in the every day experience of young American children. Paul H Brookes Pub. 1995. P.268

2. https://www.thenationalliteracyinstitute.com/2024-2025-literacy-statistics

3. http://endoftheamericandream.com/archives/dumb-as-a-rock-you-will-be-absolutely-amazed-at-the-things-that-u-s-high-school-student

4. dailymail.co.uk/news/article-2159174/LEAF-survey-One-young-adults-think

5. http://timesofindia.indiatimes.com/world/us/1-in-4-Americans-unaware-that-Earth-circles-Sun-Poll/articleshow/30421804.cm

6. Johnston.I The ipaper/The Independent 20th Jan. 2014 No.983

7. http://www.bullittcountyhistory.com/bchistory/schoolexam1912.html

8. Marwich,A. The Sixties: Cultural Revolution in Britain, France, Italy and the United States. Oxford Uni. Press 1998.

9. Dewey. D. Individuality, Equality and Superiority. New Republic 33 Dec 13 1922.

10. Feuerstein.R & Rand .Y. Mediated Learning Experiences: An outline of the proximal etiology for differential development of cognitive functions. International Understanding. L. Gold Fein (ed.) 1974

11. Murray,C & Herrnstein,R The Bell Curve:Intelligence & Class Structure in American Life. Freepress 1994.

12. Andersen,R. The Hidden Secrets of Intelligence. The Moving Quill. 2014.p.4

13. Risley,T. Hart, B. Meaningful differences in the everyday experiences of young American children. Brookes Publishing Company. 1995.

14. Wilson,W. High School Teachers Association of New York. 1909, Vol **3**, pp.19-31

15. Anderson.M. Intelligence and Development: A Cognitive Theory. Blackwell 1992. p.41

16. Axness,M. Lifelong Lessons from the Womb. ICPA. http://icpa4kids.org/fr/Wellness-Articles/lifelong-lessons-from-the-womb/Toutes-les-pages.html

17. Feuerstein.R. Rand,Y.Hoffman M.B, Miller.R Instrumental Enrichment. Scott, Foresman & Co. 1980.

18. Bayley. N Mental Growth during the first 3 years. Genetic Psychology Monographs. 1933. 14 p1-92 // Kelly.M.F. & Surbeck.E The History of Pre-school Assessment in the Psycho- Educational Assessment of Pre School Children. (ed) Paget.K.D. & Bracken,A. Grune & Stratton.N.Y. 1983..

19. Gardner,H. Frames of Mind. BasicBooks. 1983.

20. Dirix.C.E, Nijhuis.J.G, Jongsma.H.W, Hornstra.G, Aspects of fetal learning and memory. Child Dev. 2009 Jul-Aug:80 (4) p.1251-8

21. Nijhuis.J.G, Dirix. C.E.H, Jongsma, H.W. Hornstra.G. Child Development. July 2009 Vol 80. Nr.4 p.12551-1258

22. H.B. Valman and J.F. Pearson. "What the fetus feels", British Medical Journal, 26 January 1980.

23. https://www.psychologytoday.com/blog/the-superhuman-mind/201211/identical-twins-are-not-genetically-identical

24. Axness.M. Pregnancy. Lifelong Lessons from the Womb. 2010. Mar.1. issue. 25 http://icpa4kids.org/fr/Wellness-Articles/lifelong-lessons-from-the-womb/Toutes-les-pages.html

25. Fiske, J. The meaning of infancy. Boston: Houghton Miffln. 1909 (originally pub. 1883). p.1

26. Chugani H.T. Behen.M.E Muzak.O Juhasz.C. Nagy.F Chugani.D.C Local Brain Functional Activity following Early Deprivation: A Study of Postinstitutionalizd Romanian Orphans. NeuroImage. 14 2001 p.1290-1301

27. www.thecommunicationtrust.org.uk

28. http://www.telegraph.co.uk/education/educationnews/8668117/ Growing-number-of-children-dont-know-their-own-name-when-starting-school.html

29. www.independent.co.uk/news/education/education-news/half-of-all-five-year-olds-are-not-ready -for-school-research-shows-9749490.html

30. Hart.B, Risley.T.R. Meaningful differences in the every day experience of young American children. Paul H Brookes Pub. 1995. P.268

31. Walker.D, Greenwood.C, Hart.B, Carta.J, Prediction of School Outcomes Based on Early Language Production and Socioeconomic Factors. Child Development. 1994 65: p.606–621.

32. Silinskas, G. Kiuru,N. Tovanen.A. Niemi.P Lerkkanen.M, Nurmi.J. Maternal Teaching of Reading and Child's Reading Skills in Grade 1. Patterns and Predictors of Positive and Negative Assocations. Learning and Individual Differences. Elsevier. 2013. 27. p54-66

33. Sandy.L.R, Education in Finland. New Hampshire Journal of Learning 2007. Vol.10.,

34. Cooper, P.J. Collins, R. & Saxby, M. The Power of Story. Melbourne: MacMillan. 1992.

35. Carlyle,R. Sunday Express 6th Sept. 2015. p.26

36. Russel,B. The Impact of Science on Society AMS Press New York 1952 p.28

37. Ouellet-Morin, I. Odgers C.L, Danese. A, Bowes. L, Shakoor. S, Papadopoulos A.S, Caspi. A, Moffitt T.E., & Arseneault.L Blunted Cortisol Responses to Stress Signal Social and Behavioral Problems Among Maltreated/ Bullied 12-Year-Old Children. Biol. Psychiatry. http://sites.duke.edu/adaptlab/files/2012/09/Oullet-Morin-et-al-2011

38. Jennings. Reflections on a Half Century of School Reform. Centre on Educational Policy. 2012. www.cep-dc.org/cfcontent_file.cfm?.

39. Baron, J. (1993). Why teach thinking? - An essay. Applied Psychology: An International Review, 42, 191-237.

40. Watson, J. B. Behaviorism (Revised edition). Chicago: University of Chicago Press. 1930 p.82

41. http://danishfolkhighschools.com/about/history

42. Dewey.J. How We Think: A restatement of the relation of reflective thinking to the educative process. D.C. Heath & Co. Massachusetts. 1933.

[43] Jackson.W. in his introduction of Dewey.J. The School and Society. Univ. of Chicago Press. Reprint. 1956.

[44] Thorndike.E.L. Animal Intelligence: Experimental Studies. Macmillan. N.Y. 1911.

[45] Thorndike.E.L. Human Learning. Appleton-Century. 1931.

[46] Kuhn.D. The Skills of Argument. Cambridge Univ. Press. 1991. p.289/290

[47] Perry. W.G., Jr. Forms of Intellectual and Ethical Development in the College Years: A Scheme. New York: Holt, Rinehart, and Winston. 1970.

[48] Hibbert. C. The English: A Social History. Guild Pub. 1987. P.694.

[49] Department of Education and Skills. Department Report 2000.2001: Age Participation Index into Higher Education. HMSO London. 2001

[50] Jennings. Reflections on a Half Century of School Reform. Centre on Educational Policy. 2012. www.cep-dc.org/cfcontent_file.cfm?

[51] Lacey.C. Hightown Grammar. Manchester Univ. Press.1970.

[52] Tzuriel.D. Paper presented to the Conference on Individual Differences and Educational Excellence. Touro College. New York 1994 March.

[53] Robinson.P. Education and Poverty. Methuen 1976.

[54] Fillmore.C.J. paper delivered to American Culture Centre. U.C. Berkeley. Feb 97.

[55] Wolfram.W, Adger.C.T & Christian.D. Dialects in Schools and Communities. Mahwah. N.J. Erlbaum 1999.

[56] Wiley.T.G "The Case of African American Language" In T.G. Wiley. Literacy and Language Diversity in the United States. Centre for applied Linguistics and Deta Systems 1996. 125-132.

[57] http://rt.com/usa/science-education-survey-americans-178/

[58] Nearing. S. The New Education: A Reviw of Progressive Educational Movements of the Day. Chicago:Row Peterson 1915 in Tyack's The One Best System.

[59] Lacey.C. Hightown Grammar. Manchester Univ. Press.1970. p49-74.

[60] Skinner.B.F. The Behavior of Organisms. Appleton-Century-Crofts. 1938.

61 Wolman.B.B. Contemporary Theories and System in Psychology. Plenum 1981.p.30

62 Auger,W.F. Rich.S.J. Curriculum theory and methods: Perspectives on learning and teaching. John Wiley& Sons 2007

63 Feuerstein.R & Hoffman.M.B Intergenerational conflict of Rights: Cultural Imposition and Self-realisation. Journal of the School of education Indiana Univ. 1982. Vol 58 No.1 p55

64 Piaget.J. Science of education and the psychology of the child. Viking Press. 1971.

65 Piaget.J. The Origins of Intelligence in Children. International Universities Press. N.Y. 1952.

66 Aguayo.R Dr.Deming: The American who taught the Japanese about Quality. Pub: Fireside 1991

67 Cornesky.R.A, McCool.S. Byrnes.L & Weber.R. Implementing Total Quality Management in Institutions of Higher Education. Atwood Publishers 1991.

68 Montessori.M. Education for Human Development. Schocken 1976

69 Donaldson.M. Children's Minds. Fontana Press. 1978.

70 Luria.A.R. The Nature of Human Conflicts. Liveright 1932.

71 Chomsky.N. Language and Mind. Harcourt Brace Jovanovitch. 1972.

72 Rose.S.A. & Blank,M, The potency of context in children's cognition: an illustration through conservation. Child Development 1974. No 45. p499-502.

73 Chugani.H.T. Development of Regional Brain Glucose Metabolism in Relation to Behavior and Plasticity. In Human Behavior and the Developing Brain (ed) Dawson.G Fischer.K.W. Guldford Pub. 1994 p. 153-175.

74 Anderson J.R. Cognitive Psychology and its Implications. Freeman 1985 p400-426.

75 Sophian.C Origins of Cognitive Skills. Lawrence Erlbaum. 1984.

76 Andersen.R "Can Children Learn Better" Pub in Denmark. Børn Kan Lære Bedre. UngTryk. 1998

77 Dewey. J. the Educational Situation. Univ. of Chicago Press 1902.

[78] Adams.R The Guardian. 2013. July 8th. http://www.guardian.co.uk/politics/2013/jul/08/michael-gove-education-curriculum

[79] http://nyhederne.tv2.dk/samfund/2015-05-13-it-kaos-rammer-9-klassernes-afgangsproever

[80] Borba, M. UnSelfie: Why Empathic Kids Succeed in Our All-About-Me World SimonandSchuster Pub. 2016

[81] http://journals.lww.com/neurologynow/Fulltext/2014/10030/Game_Theory__How_do_video_games_affect_the.17.aspx

[82] https://www.princeton.edu/futureofchildren/publications/docs/10_02_05.pdf

[83] http://www.dailymail.co.uk/sciencetech/article-2067607/Violent-games-DO-alter-brain--effect-visible-MRI-scans-just-week.html

[84] http://journals.lww.com/neurologynow/Fulltext/2014/10030/Game_Theory__How_do_video_games_affect_the.17.aspx

[85] http://journals.lww.com/neurologynow/Fulltext/2014/10030/Game_Theory__How_do_video_games_affect_the.17.aspx

[86] Mason.L, Ariasi.N, & Boldrin. A. Epistemic beliefs in action: Spontaneous reflections about knowledge and knowing during online information searching and their influence on learning. /Learning and Instruction. 2011. Jan. 21 p.137-151.

[87] Barzilai.S, & Zohar. A, Epistemic thinking in action: Evaluating and integrating online sources.Cognition and Instruction. 2012 30(1) p.39–85.

[88] https://www.ideatovalue.com/crea/nickskillicorn/2016/08/evidence-children-become-less-creative-time-fix/

[89] Iserbyt. C.T. The Deliberate Dumbing Down of America. Pub.Last Century Media. 2022.

[90] Johard.M, New Study: Gen AI could affect 90% of all jobs. Cognizant Blog. 22nd January. 2024 https://www.cognizant.com/se/en/ 2 insights/blog/articles/new-study-gen-ai-could-affect-90-percent-of-all-jobs#:~:text=Joint Oxford Economics/Cognizant study,work,new world" report.

[91] Borba, M. UnSelfie: Why Empathic Kids Succeed in Our All-About-Me World SimonandSchuster Pub. 2016

[92] Maynard. G, The Daily Express: re Interparcel study. 2015 7th March.

www.ingramcontent.com/pod-product-compliance
Lightning Source LLC
Chambersburg PA
CBHW020418010526
44118CB00010B/307